DATE DUE
PIONEERING
MICHIGAN

D

PIONEERING MICHIGAN

by Eric Freedman

A&M

Altwerger and Mandel Publishing Company
Franklin, Michigan

ISBN 1-878005-23-5 Cl
ISBN 1-878005-24-3 Pb

First Edition 1992

Designed by Mary Primeau

To my wife Mary Ann Sipher and our
children, Ian and Cara,
who pioneered to Michigan
with me in 1984

Contents

CONTENTS

Acknowledgments

This book would not have been possible without much help and cooperation from others. My thanks to *The Detroit News*, for permission to reprint portions of articles I wrote for the Michigan Sesquicentennial and to use photos from its collection. The staffs of the Library of Michigan, State Archives and Bureau of History were always helpful, with particular appreciation for the efforts of photo archivist John Curry, librarian Carole Callard and editor Saralee Howard-Filler. Volunteers and staff at museums, historical societies and genealogical societies across Michigan assisted with research and finding illustrations. My children Ian and Cara assisted with some typing.

Special thanks to my *Detroit News* colleague George Weeks, author of Stewards of the State, whose avid interest in Michigan history motivated me to undertake this project.

Of course, this book would have been impossible without the cooperation of descendants of Sesquicentennial pioneers.

Map of Michigan's 83 counties.

Proud of their own heritages, these women and men graciously shared with me family pictures and information about their ancestors.

Introduction

Early Michigan history is far more than a list of dates and famous names to memorize. It is the saga of people, mostly ordinary people, who shaped a state and its societies. Not everything they did to survive or to prosper proved wise, at least in retrospect, but any failings were human shortcomings, produced by the same mixed and conflicting emotions and impulses that we feel today —fear, hunger, audacity, ambition, love, greed, courage, imagination, comfort, caution and insecurity.

To understand the forces that made Michigan, we need to look at the individuals and families involved, not just at the institutions and politics and economic forces of their times. Often the stories are best told in their own words —journals and letters —or in the words and memories of their descendants.

On Aug. 28, 1834, a young lawyer named Jefferson Gage Thurber wrote to his in-laws in distant New Hampshire about a cholera plague devastating Detroit. Thurber had settled 37 miles away in Monroe the previous year:

> You most likely have heard that 'the arrow that flieth by day; the pestilence that walketh in darkness; and the destruction that wasteth in noon-day' is amongst us. In Detroit there is a population of about 5,000 souls. And within the last 20 days there have died of the cholera about 300 persons. Its malignity has however abated, and for the last three days but few deaths have occurred. I have seen no account when the ravages of the Destroyer have been so seriously felt.
>
> With the exception of a few cases of cholera, our Village has been very healthy. The future, we cannot see, but from the very healthy location of our Village and its elevation, we are in hopes that the Scourge will fall lightly upon us.
>
> If you have the disease among you, do your duty, pursue your regular habits, be cheerful, take no medicine unless you are sick.

Hervey Parke of Pontiac set out with a surveying party in 1821. This is his recollection of an expedition in the Flint River area:

> We had no tents, only an old second-hand tarpulin which had been laid aside as useless for hatchway service. In the absence of a kneading trough, our cook made use of this canvas to mix his bread. This was unfortunate for on our first visit to the trading house some swine, attracted to the adhering dough, nearly devoured and destroyed it and we had no cover besides our blankets.

Looking back, the event reflects a blend of absurdity, anger, discomfort and frustration. But Parke also recalled crossing paths in the wilderness with another surveying crew in a situation that lacked the irony or touch of levity of the pig incident. "The men," he recalled, were "utterly refusing to continue longer on account of the suffering they had endured from mosquitoes, both men and horses being weak from loss of blood and want of rest."

Mosquitoes and fatigue —the image of that combination is tangible to us more than a century and a half later.

An historical account of Japheth Fisher's experiences as an early Eaton County settler provides another human perspective on frontier life, Fisher was known to attend frontier logging bees barefooted:

> To test the toughness of his feet, (neighbor) Jim Taggert would station or push him on a large bull-thistle. Japheth, with his full rosy cheeks laughing and talking, would seem perfectly unconscious of the fact his bare foot was crushing the fangs of one of those savage thistles, and that all were looking to see him either wince, or back down, or move his foot to some more comfortable place.

And Theodore E. Potter recalled his childhood on the Washtenaw County farm his parents had purchased before statehood. He was injured at the age of $3^1/_2$:

> I tried to go up the stairs on a ladder, fell and caught one leg between the rounds and broke it above the knee, from which I suffered so much pain that to stop my crying my brother, who did not know my leg was broken, carried me from one bed to another, my leg dangling, and it was four hours before my father returned. He started on foot for Saline, five miles away, to get a doctor, and by the time he came my broken leg was very badly swollen.

The genesis of this book is an assignment I received from an editor late in 1986, while I worked as a reporter in the Lansing Bureau of *The Detroit News*. As part of the impending celebration of the 150th anniversary of statehood in 1987, the Library of Michigan and the Michigan Genealogical Council designed a Sesquicentennial Pioneer program to honor people who could prove their ancestors were in Michigan by 1837, the year it became the 26th state.

One editor suggested a weekly series of articles profiling some of those pioneer families. A second editor, who heard the idea, wrote a memo to a third editor, who passed it on to a fourth who, in turn handed it to a fifth. That fifth editor handed the memo to me, saying, "Just do it for a few weeks and we'll find somebody to take over after that."

Nobody took over, so I wrote more than 60 family profiles that were published between late 1986 and early 1988. In the process, I scoured hundreds of Sesquicentennial Pioneer applications at the Library of Michigan for interesting —not necessarily "important" —settlers, interviewed at least one descendant of each pioneer I wrote about, researched books, maps and articles about Michigan's past, and sent *Detroit News* photographers across the state.

The legacies of the people I wrote about are recorded in family traditions, local churches, farms, community organizations and inscriptions on tombstones, as well as in historic archives, libraries and yellowed government records. A number of the pioneers' proud descendants took the time to send me more material including excerpts from family histories and diaries, newspaper obituaries and copies of faded letters and documents.

So as you read *Pioneering Michigan*, you'll come across a handful of names that appear in standard history books. But don't look in the textbooks for the names of Cobmosa or Sarah Webb or Peter Van Tifflin or Francis Bienvenu dit DeLisle or most of the others profiled here. You won't find them. These are primarily the ordinary people who pioneered Michigan, from the Native Americans who had called this place home for centuries to those who journeyed into the unknown from distant places, some speaking no English.

As a 19th century historian wrote —with perhaps some overgeneralization —about southwestern Michigan settlers:

> They were a cheerful, contented people, whose wants were few and those easily supplied; hospitable to a fault, the latch strings of their cabin doors had knots in the end and were always out.

No one was refused accommodation. . . . As a general thing their chief business was to live, having but little propensity for speculation.

These were women and men who searched for opportunities and changes and found satisfactions and frustrations. They worked, raised children, explored a rapidly changing world and lived modest lives.

The Road to Statehood

The price was Toledo.

But amid promise and confidence — and despite economic uncertainty — Michigan finally won statehood on Jan. 26, 1837, when President Andrew Jackson signed a one-page bill "to admit the State of Michigan into the Union, upon an equal footing with the Original States."

On a national level, the delicate balance between slave and free states was restored because pro-slavery Arkansas had been admitted to the Union a year earlier. On a local level, it meant Michigan could share in any U.S. Treasury surplus and collect 5 percent of the profits from the sale of government land within its borders.

Toledo?

Congress approved the statehood law after several days of vigorous debate, and only after the president reported Michigan's willingness — reluctant willingness, it must be emphasized

Twenty fourth

CONGRESS OF THE UNITED STATES;

At the second Session,

Begun and held at the City of Washington, on Monday, the *fifth* day of December, one thousand eight hundred and *thirty-six*

AN ACT

to admit the State of Michigan into the Union, upon an equal footing with the original States.

Whereas, in pursuance of the act of Congress of June the fifteenth, eighteen hundred and thirty-six, entitled "An act to establish the northern boundaries of the State of Ohio, and to provide for the admission of the State of Michigan into the Union upon the conditions therein expressed," a convention of delegates, elected by the people of the said State of Michigan, for the sole purpose of giving their assent to the boundaries of the said State of Michigan as described, declared, and established, in and by the said act, did, on the fifteenth of December, eighteen hundred and thirty-six, assent to the provisions of said act, therefore: Be it enacted by the Senate and House of Representatives of the United States of America in Congress assembled, That the State of Michigan shall be one, and is hereby declared to be one, of the United States of America, and admitted into the Union on an equal footing with the original States, in all respects whatever. Section 2. And be it further enacted, That the Secretary of the Treasury, in carrying into effect the thirteenth and fourteenth sections of the act of the twenty third of June, eighteen hundred and thirty-six, entitled "An act to regulate the deposites of the public money," shall consider the State of Michigan as being one of the United States.

James K. Polk Speaker of the House of Representatives.

Richard M. Johnson { Vice President of the United States, and President of the Senate.

approved this 26 January 1837 —

Andrew Jackson

20

The statehood law. On Jan. 26, 1837, President Andrew Jackson signed this bill *(opposite)* granting statehood to Michigan: "Be it enacted by the Senate and the House of Representatives of the United States of America in Congress assembled that the State of Michigan shall be one, and is hereby declared to be one, of the United States of America, and admitted into the Union on an equal footing with the original states, in all respects whatever." The president's action marked the culmination of a concerted push for statehood by the territory's expanding number of settlers. *State Archives of Michigan*

—to recognize Ohio's ownership of the 520-square-mile Toledo Strip. Because Ohio already was a state, its U.S. senators and representatives were able to hold hostage Michigan's bid for statehood until they won what they wanted — sovereignty over the disputed land, including what would become the economically vital Lake Erie port of Toledo at the outlet of the Maumee River.

It was a painful compromise. After all, Territorial Gov. Stevens T. Mason had declared, "If the demand of Ohio is tamely submitted to, what becomes of the rights of the states? Surrender once to the sordid grasp of a state seeking empire or power, and the period may arrive when one portion of the nation appealing to their own strength will prescribe laws for their weaker neighbors."

In fact, war — of a sort — had broken out in 1835 when Mason and Ohio Gov. Robert Lucas marched their rival militias to a face-to-face border confrontation with troops camped on opposite banks of the Maumee. At a 1905 memorial ceremony in Detroit, Rev. Riley C. Crawford recalled how the militia "had marched at the sound of my fife to Toledo, all in one day."

In her autobiography, the governor's sister Emily V. Mason related this war song of the day:

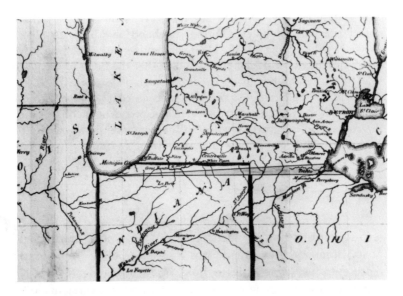

The Toledo Strip. The shaded area of this map marks the 520-square-mile Toledo Strip along the southern boundary of Michigan Territory. The centerpiece of a heated political and quasi-military dispute, it delayed and threatened to derail statehood. The boundary had been established in the Northwest Ordinance of 1787 as a line east of the southern tip of Lake Michigan. An 1817 federal survey by a former Ohio governor put the area in Ohio, but another survey in 1818 placed it in Michigan. Just 19 days before President Andrew Jackson signed the Michigan statehood bill, Ohio incorporated and combined two communities in the strip, Port Lawrence and Vistula, and renamed them as the new municipality "Toledo." Congress gave Michigan the western three-quarters of the Upper Peninsula as a consolation prize. *State Archives of Michigan*

Old Lucas gave his order all for to hold a court
But Stevens Thomson Mason he thought he'd have some sport;
He called upon the Wolverines and them for to go
To meet the rebel Lucas, his court to overthrow.

Stevens T. Mason. Political power came early to Stevens T. Mason, an ambitious man for ambitious times in an ambitious place. Born in Virginia, he found himself territorial secretary at age 19 after his father John T. Mason —who had held the post —persuaded President Andrew Jackson to appoint him in 1831. Jackson ousted Mason in September 1835, but he was elected territorial governor a month later at age 24 and reelected in 1837, thus overseeing the turbulent transition period into statehood. He was described as "of slender, flexible and elegant figure, with small aristocratic hands and feet. His face was full, his forehead was not high, but rather broad, and his brown, waving hair fell in rich clusters about his head." He pushed for free public education, internal improvements such as canals, roads and railroads, and training programs for prisoners. Mason had a temper, however, and reportedly punched an editor who called him the "Boy Governor." Just as his career began early, so too did it end. Michigan was beset by a national economic depression and its banking system collapsed, dooming any additional political aspirations he may have held. He moved to New York City after leaving office and died there at age 30 of either pneumonia or "suppressed scarlet fever." In 1905, his remains were returned to Detroit for reinterment in Capitol Park, the site of the territorial Capitol and the first seat of state government. *State Archives of Michigan*

There was virtually no bloodshed, however. Some Ohio officials and surveyors were arrested by the Michigan forces in the contested area, and a Michigan deputy sheriff was fatally stabbed with a penknife by an Ohioan during a tavern brawl.

The "war" ended when Jackson ousted Mason from office and the Michigan militia commander disbanded the territorial troops.

Jackson's signature capped a lengthy struggle by the people of rapidly growing Michigan Territory. Their first request for statehood came in an 1832 petition to Congress, but neither the Senate nor the House of Representatives acted on it. Mason then initiated a census in 1834 that counted more than the 60,000 inhabitants required for statehood under the Northwest Ordinance of 1787.

The Territorial Council called an 1835 constitutional convention in Detroit to design a state government. Delegates adopted and the voters approved a Constitution and Bill of Rights. Congress agreed in June 1836 to admit Michigan once it surrendered its claim to the Toledo Strip. One of Michigan's few congressional allies in the debate was former President John Quincy Adams of Massachusetts, who was serving in the House of Representatives. Adams declared in a three-hour speech, "Never in the course of my life have I known controversy of which all the right was so clear on one side, and all the power so overwhelmingly on the other."

With that condition imposed by Congress and the White House, statehood seemed assured —until territorial delegates met in Ann Arbor in September 1836 and refused to yield to Ohio. A second convention was held in Ann Arbor on a bitterly cold December day. Delegates to the "Frostbitten Convention" yielded to the politically inevitable and eliminated the final stumbling block to statehood.

In exchange, Michigan accepted from Congress the western three-quarters of the little-explored Upper Peninsula. That domain had been called a "sterile region on the shores of Lake Superior, destined to remain forever a wilderness." A Detroit newspaper characterized it as "the region of perpetual snows — the ultima Thule of our national domain on the North." In addition, the area had been regarded as part of Wisconsin Territory, and its relatively few residents were opposed to joining Michigan, preferring that Congress establish the entire Upper Peninsula as a separate Territory of Huron. On the more upbeat side, territorial U.S. Sen. Lucius Lyon — who originally thought little of the Upper Peninsula — predicted that it would prove worth $40 million in a decade, and another observer remarked that "the whitefish of Lake Superior might be a fair offset for the lost bull-frog pastures of the Maumee."

The battle for statehood reflects several common themes interwoven in Michigan history — opportunity, challenge, conflict and exploitation.

Native Americans came to Michigan at least 11,000 years ago.

An Ojibway legend tells how, long ago when the world was younger, the Ojibway were among the Seven Fires, the seven tribes of the Algonquin nation that lived along the coast of the Great Salt Sea, or Atlantic Ocean. An Algonquin priest prophesized the destructive advent of the whites and revealed that Gitchi Manitou, the Great Spirit, wanted them to move toward the setting sun until they reached the Place of the Turtle. Six of the seven tribes started west, traveling over the passing years along the St. Lawrence River to Lake Ontario, past Niagara Falls to Lake Erie, along the Detroit River and into Lake Huron. Most of the tribes settled at the various stopping places, but the Ojibway pushed on to Sault Ste. Marie and then to Michilmackinac, the turtle-shaped island between lakes Huron and Michigan. Some stayed there while others continued north, eventually settling along Lake Superior.

By the time the first Europeans arrived in Michigan in the 1620s, the area was home to the Ojibway or Chippewa, Ottawa, Potawatomi, Miami and Menominee tribes — all members of the Algonquin nation — and to the Wyandot, related to the Iroquois.

The mid-17th century began a period of European influence

25

Lucius Lyon. Vermont-born Lucius Lyon, had been a surveyor, land speculator and deputy surveyor general before his election as a territorial delegate to Congress in 1832. By the time Congress debated the fate of statehood for Michigan a few years later, he had risen to one of the two non-voting territorial U.S. senators. When the western three-quarters of the Upper Peninsula was offered in exchange for the contested Toledo Strip, he initially belittled the swap, joking that Michigan would use the northern area merely to "supply ourselves

now and then with a little bear meat for a delicacy." He soon changed his mind, forseeing that the Upper Peninsula would become a profitable asset for the new state. After leaving Washington, he moved to Grand Rapids to monitor his salt mining and real estate interests. In 1845 he was named U.S. Surveyor General for Michigan, Indiana and, perhaps ironically, Ohio –a presidential appointment he resisted until the post was moved from Cincinnati to Detroit. *State Archives of Michigan*

and confrontation, starting with the travels of French explorer Etienne Brule in northern Michigan and the founding of the first mission in Sault Ste. Marie by Father Jacques Marquette, a French Jesuit priest who spoke a number of Indian dialects. Voyageurs and fur traders followed.

The British cast covetous glances at the abounding natural resources and wary looks at their traditional enemies, the French. French military outposts were established, including Fort St. Joseph in Niles, Fort Miami in St. Joseph, another Fort

Jacques Marquette. Father Jacques Marquette, the best known of Michigan missionaries, came from France to Quebec in 1666 and worked with Brother Luis Boeme to open a chapel and mission in Sault Ste. Marie two years later. In 1673, he set out by canoe from St. Ignace on a five-month, 2,500-mile journey from Lake Michigan to the Mississippi River and back. He wrote in his journal: "The Joy that we felt at being selected for This Expedition animated our Courage, and rendered the labor of paddling from morning to night agreeable to us. And because We were going to seek Unknown countries, We took every precaution in our power, so that, if our Undertaking were hazardous, it should not be foolhardy." The expedition was successful, but Marquette died two years later when he was only 33. A biographer described him as a "17th century man doing his duty for God and king." *State Archives of Michigan*

St. Joseph in Port Huron, Fort Michilmackinac in Mackinaw City and Fort Ponchartrain in Detroit.

The French and Indian War left Britain with sovereignty over former French holdings in Michigan. London's control over the region was not without problems though. In 1763, Chief Pontiac and 300 Ottawa warriers besieged Fort Detroit for five months, yielding only when the British forces received badly needed supplies and accepting a British promise to block further white settlements in the west. In a moving speech of submission to the British commander, Pontiac said:

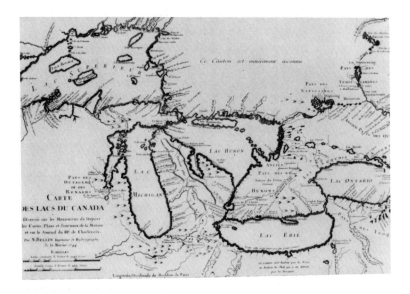

Michigan in 1744. This French map depicts Michigan and the Great Lakes in 1744, before Great Britain wrested control through its victory in the French and Indian War. *State Archives of Michigan*

Father, we have all smoked out of this pipe of peace. It is your children's pipe; and as the war is all over, and the Great Spirit and Giver of Light, who has made this earth and everything therein, has brought us all together this day for mutual good, I declare to all nations that I have settled my peace with you before I came here, and now deliver my pipe to be sent to Sir William Johnson (an Irish-born New Yorker who had been adopted by the Mohawks and became the British Indian agent for nothern tribes) that he may know I have made peace, and taken the King of England for my father, in the presence of all nations now assembled; and whenever any of those nations go to visit him, they may smoke out of it with him in peace.

28

Britain kept Michigan throughout the American Revolution but ceded the region to the newly independent nation in the 1783 treaty that ended that war.

Although France and England were the principal colonial powers in the area, even the Spanish flag flew over Michigan — briefly. That happened in 1781, when Spanish raiders allied with the Americans seized Fort St. Joseph in Niles from the British and held it for a single day.

Michigan's fate was left up to Congress in the distant east, and its borders would be shaped and reshaped several times in the decades to follow. The Ordinance of 1787 included it with Ohio, Wisconsin, Illinois, Indiana and part of Minnesota as the Northwest Territory. In 1803 it was made part of Indiana Territory. And in 1805 it became a territory of its own with a small portion of the Upper Peninsula.

The War of 1812 touched but did not devastate Michigan. Territorial Gov. William Hull surrendered Detroit to the British, making it the only major U.S. city ever to be fully occupied by an enemy during wartime. Ten days after the surrender, Hull defended his decision in a letter to Secretary of War William Eustis:

> A large portion of the brave and gallant officers and men I commanded would cheerfully have contested until the last cartridge had been expended, and the bayonets worn to the sockets. I could not consent to the useless sacrifice of such brave men, when I knew it was impossible for me to sustain my situation. It was impossible in the nature of things that an army could have been furnished with the necessary supplies of provision, military stores, clothing and comforts for the sick, or pack horses, through a wilderness of 200 miles, filled with hostile savages.

However, Lewis Cass, a colonel under Hull and soon to become territorial governor himself, took an opposite view of his commander's surrender, asserting that he and the other colonels

29

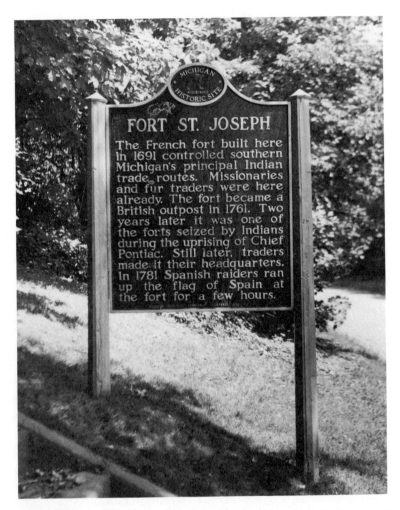

French forts. The French sought to maintain control of Michigan and its economic resources through a series of strategically placed forts. Fort Miami, (*opposite*) on Lake Michigan at the mouth of the St. Joseph River, served as a base for western explorations by Robert Cavelier, Sieurde la Salle. Twenty miles away in Niles, Fort St. Joseph dominated trade routes between southern Michigan and the Indians. *Michigan Travel Commission*

FORT MIAMI

Here in November, 1679, on the Miami River, as the St. Joseph was then called, La Salle, the French explorer, built a fort as a base for his western explorations. Here he awaited the *Griffin*, the upper lakes' first ship. When the ill-fated vessel did not come he made his way on foot to Canada through lower Michigan's uncharted wilderness. He returned in 1681 to prepare his great push down the Mississippi. A decade later the French built Fort St. Joseph, some 20 miles upriver near Niles.

Fort Michilmackinac. First the French and then the British maintained a fort in what is now Mackinaw City, on the mainland overlooking the strategic Straits of Mackinac that connects lakes Michigan and Huron. Most of the British garrison was killed in a Chippewa uprising in 1763, but the fort was reoccupied until 1781, when it was abandoned in favor of the new fort on Mackinac Island. Fort Michilmackinac was reconstructed as a state historic park. *Michigan Travel Commission*

General William Hull, a Revolutionary War veteran and territorial governor since 1805, had been placed in command of the North Western Army with responsibility for American forts in Michigan, Illinois and Fort Wayne during the War of 1812. The Connecticut native surrendered Detroit without a shot to the British in August 1812 and was taken prisoner of war. After his release, he was court-martialed and sentenced to die for cowardice, unofficerlike conduct and neglect of duty although acquitted of treason. He was reprieved by President James Madison from execution by firing squad. The daughter of a pioneer later wrote, "My father was William Scott and was baptized 'William Hull Scott,' but after Hull's disgraceful surrender of Detroit, the name Hull was cut out of the family record in the Bible." However, a sympathetic biographer wrote, "Of course it was not intended that the sentence should be inflicted. All they wanted was a victim, and to put him to death might make him a martyr." *State Archives of Michigan*

know and feel that no circumstance in our situation, none in that of our enemy, can excuse a capitulation so dishonorable and unjustifiable. This too is the universal sentiment among the troops; and I shall be surprised to learn that there is one man who thinks it was necessary to sheath his sword, or lay down his musket.

Hull was court-martialed for his actions in 1814 but granted a presidential reprieve from a death sentence.

Battle of River Raisin memorial. The Battle of River Raisin in Monroe during the War of 1812 was the largest battle ever fought in Michigan. As the Monroe Democrat described it, this monument was dedicated in 1872 "to mark the resting place of the Kentucky soldiers who fell in the vain attempt to rescue the defenseless settlers on the River Raisin, as well as to commemorate their bravery and voluntary sacrifice." *Christine Kull, Monroe County Historical Commission*

In addition to seizing Detroit, the British captured the American fort and its 62 soldiers on Mackinac Island without a shot.

After the British rousted the outnumbered Americans in the January 1813 Battle of the River Raisin in Monroe, many of the survivors were slaughtered by the victors' Indian allies. As a memorial marker relates, "Forced to surrender, though promised British protection, the prisoners left unguarded were attacked and killed."

It proved to be the most important battle of the war in Michigan, and author-lawyer-politician Levi Bishop later described it this way:

35

Fort Mackinac. During the American Revolution, the British lieutenant governor and commander of the garrison, Patrick Sinclair, feared that American rebels would attack Fort Michilmackinac on the mainland. So in 1779, the British began to build a replacement atop a hill on Mackinac Island, overlooking the harbor. Work was completed in 1781. The fort is now a popular tourist attraction. *Michigan Travel Commission*

And Raisin's banks are heaped with dead,
And Raisin's flood is dyed with red;
Brave warriors find a lowly bed —
The soldier's honored tomb.

Though victory we cannot boast
Yet held the field at any cost
Oh, yield it not till it has lost
Its very last defender.

The Americans reentered Detroit 19 days after Lt. Oliver Hazard Perry's critical naval victory over the British fleet in the

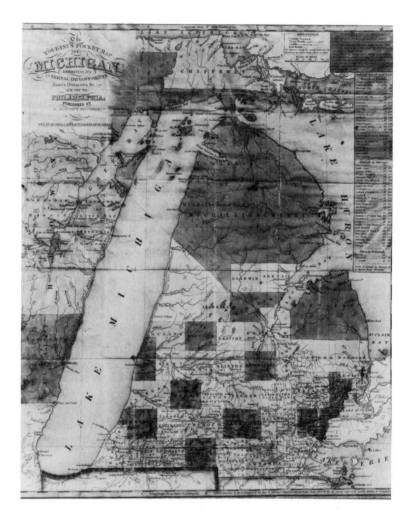

Michigan shortly before statehood. The Tourist's Pocket Map of Michigan was published in Philadelphia and shows the territory shortly before statehood, including its "internal improvements" and "roads distances" but without most of the Upper Peninsula. Included is a listing of steam boat routes which brought thousands of settlers from the western terminus of the Erie Canal at Buffalo across Lake Erie to Michigan. *State Archives of Michigan*

September 1813 Battle of Lake Erie. Adequate food, medical supplies and shelter were lacking, however, and soon an estimated 700 American troops were dead of a cholera-like epidemic.

Peace returned. Back in Washington, Congress expanded Michigan Territory westward and northward in 1818, adding the remainder of the Upper Peninsula, Wisconsin and part of Minnesota. Then it transferred most of the Upper Peninsula to Wisconsin Territory.

Finally, with the the ultimate resolution of the political controversy, Michigan lost the Toledo Strip but ended up with the entire Upper Peninsula and statehood.

A few weeks before final congressional approval was achieved, Mason had looked ahead in a way that recent pioneers would find comforting, for his thoughts reflected their own aspirations for the future. The words Mason spoke were, after all, representative of their own motives and wishes and dreams, even if many of them had not yet—and would not—achieve the prosperity and success of which he boasted:

> The tide of emigration is rapidly extending its course to the remotest borders of the state; unprecedented health has blessed the habitations of the people; abundant harvests have crowned the exertions of the agriculturist; our cities and villages are thronging with an active and enterprising population; and not withstanding the embarrassments which have surrounded us in our relations to the federal Union, social order has been preserved, and the majesty of the law has been supreme.

Who Pioneered Michigan?
And Why?

About 1827, my father, being smitten with the Michigan fever, came to investigate reports of this, then a territory and now a great state. Being favorably impressed with what he saw, he returned to New York State for his family, and in June 1835 he landed in Detroit with all his earthly possessions, consisting of a few household goods and a family of six children.

Alden N. Giddings was 13 when his parents, Crocker and Orpha Giddings, made their journey west. It was 62 years later that he described his memories at a meeting of the Oakland County Pioneer Society. He talked not only of settlement but of life on the frontier. On education, for example, he recalled, "Most of the knowledge then was disseminated from log school houses. These schools were presided over by teachers whose leading and sometimes only qualification was the use of birch or hickory."

Crocker and Orpha Giddings, like most early settlers in Michigan, were undoubtedly dreamers, searchers for a new life, willing to swap the familiar for the enticement of the unknown, venturing to sparsely populated — and sometimes unpopulated — regions.

They came alone, or with families, or accompanied by a few

James Witherell. Revolutionary War veteran James Witherell was born in Massachusetts and studied medicine and law. After the war, he moved to Vermont, where he won a seat in the U.S. House of Representatives. He left Congress in 1808 to accept a presidential appointment to the Michigan territorial Supreme Court. He served in the War of 1812, then became territorial secretary and acting  governor. His son Benjamin served in the state House of Representatives and Senate and was a Wayne County prosecutor, University of Michigan regent and state Supreme Court justice. *Michigan as a Province, Territory & State, 1906*

friends. They were farmers and merchants, lawyers and entrepreneurs, teachers and loggers, missionaries and fur traders.

Some early settlers were veterans of the Revolution and War of 1812, motivated to emigrate by the availability of government bounty land in the territory.

Among the Revolutionary soldiers who took advantage of the bounty land was Stephen Mack, a colonel in the Vermont colonial troops, who helped found Pontiac and became a prominent Detroit merchant.

Another Revolutionary fighter-turned-settler was James Witherell, who gave up a congressional seat from Vermont in 1808 to accept a presidential appointment as a judge on the Michigan territorial Supreme Court. When Witherell commanded a military unit during the War of 1812 to defend Detroit, he "broke his sword to escape the mortification of relinquishing it to the enemy" when the city was surrendered to the British by Gen. William Hull, the territorial governor. Later, Witherell himself became secretary and then acting governor of the territory, dying the year after statehood was achieved.

The largest proportion of pre-statehood arrivals came from New York, followed by settlers from Canada, various eastern states and Europe. They hailed from places like Batavia in New York, Dorgheda in Ireland, Quebec in Canada, Isle of Man in the British Isles and New Haven in Connecticut. Meanwhile, southerners in search of opportunities were more likely to stay in Indiana, Ohio and Illinois, where they found fertile farmland before reaching Michigan.

Many traveled west by way of the Erie Canal, which had opened in 1825. Its popularity gave birth to a traditional American folk song: "You can always tell your neighbor, you can always tell your pal, if you've ever been on the Erie Canal." From the canal's western terminus at Buffalo, pioneers crossed Lake Erie, where steamboat service had begun in 1818 with *Walk-in-the-Water*.

In fact, a number of future Michiganians helped build the Erie Canal, with or without an awareness that they were opening the doors to their own westward futures. One of them was Irish-born Peter Fagan who worked on the canal, then traveled to Oakland County. He would later help construct the Detroit & Saginaw Turnpike, a key military road and another path for expansion deeper into the frontier.

The new arrivals also constructed the railroads, roads and canals that pierced the wilderness.

For example, English-born James Henry Snook undertook to build a 1½-mile segment of the Clinton-Kalamazoo Canal, an ambitious "internal improvement" to connect lakes Michigan and St. Clair by way of the Clinton and Kalamazoo rivers. Snook and other contractors hired separate work crews to dig each segment, and one historian described how "mushroom

41

Along the Erie Canal. The Erie Canal was the pipeline for settlers to Michigan Territory. Completed in 1825, the 363-mile canal linked Buffalo on Lake Erie to Albany on the Hudson River. It eliminated a major obstacle to immigration by providing relatively easy and affordable transportation for settlers, their possessions and their livestock. From Buffalo, immigrants generally traveled by steamer to Detroit, where they could remain or opt to fan outward across the state-to-be. The canal was the principal reason why New Yorkers and New Englanders accounted for such a high proportion of Michigan pioneers. At the same time, it provided Michigan with a convenient way to ship its goods to eastern markets. *State Archives of Michigan*

towns sprange up to accommodate the little army of workers and their streets were the scenes of gambling, drinking and robbery."

In an unusual move, Snook refused to allow his 35–50 workers to drink liquor. "In those days it was generally believed that such work could not be done unless the men were furnished

Walk-in-the-Water. The first steamship on the upper Great Lakes above Niagara Falls was *Walk-in-the-Water*, named for a Wyandot leader who fought the War of 1812 on the British side. Using sails to supplement its steam power, the ship first reached Detroit from Buffalo in August 1818, signaling the advent of water travel to the territory. Passage cost $18 in a cabin, $7 in steerage. The following year it also traveled to Mackinac Island and Green Bay under Capt. Job Fish. After being wrecked in an 1821 storm, its machinery was salvaged and installed in a new steamship, the Superior. In 1825, two more ships were launched to serve travelers across Lake Erie. *Dossin Great Lakes Museum*

regular rations of whiskey," a Macomb County history relates. Doubters predicted that Snook's task would fail, but because of his "just and urbane treatment of the men, the 'temperance job' became very popular with workmen, and none ever left it because whiskey or whiskey drinkers were not employed."

Potawatomi deeds. Through a series of treaties, deeds and agreements (*opposite and following page*), Michigan tribes negotiated away or sold most of their land. In this 1786 deed in English, the "chiefs of the Potawatomi Nation of the Detroit" gave land along the River Raisin to "our friend Pierre Labady." The document also says that "for the good friendship, which we bear him, we light for him a fire of peace and tranquility warranting to him from now and forever the said piece of land herein presented that he may enjoy it without any hindrance whatever." The deed in French, dated July 28, 1780, gives land in River Rouge to "notre ami" — our friend — Jacques Godfrey. *State Archives of Michigan (deed in English) & The Detroit News (deed in French)*

However, financial problems and the spread of the railroads prevented completion of the entire canal. The portions that were done fell into a "state of picturesque ruin."

From a blacksmith shop on the banks of the Clinton River, Charles Callow forged the first rail line from his adopted city of Pontiac to Detroit. Callow had learned blacksmithing on the Isle of Man in the Irish Sea, where he was born, and brought his skills to Oakland County before statehood.

Some skeptics believed Michigan would never grow populous enough to join the Union. In 1787, James Monroe explored the area and reported, "A great part of the Territory is miserably poor, especially near Lakes Michigan and Erie. The districts, therefore, in which these fall will never contain sufficient number of inhabitants to entitle them to membership in the confederacy."

The official non-Indian population rose from 3,100 in 1810 to 174,619 in 1837. Without improved means of travel to and within Michigan, the territory would not have achieved statehood and Monroe's comment would have been regarded as foresighted rather than shortsighted.

When the Europeans arrived in 1620, there were an estimated 15,000 to 20,000 Native Americans scattered within what are

Nous les Chefs de la nation des Poutéouatamis après avoir délibéré sur l'état actuel des terres que nous laissons incultes, depuis longtems, de l'avis et consentement général de la nation, avons déterminé d'en donner une portion à nôtre amy Jacques Godfroy père. Contenant trois arpents de front sur la rivière rouge à main gauche en montant ladite rivière laquelle portera sa profondeur jusqu'aux terres des p. p. Conna frères tenant d'un côté à Isidore chesne, et de l'autre côté à menich Labady. et pour la bonne et sincere amitié que luy portons nous luy allumons un feu de paix de tranquilité en luy garantissant dès à présent et à toujours ses hoirs et ayant cause de la susditte portion de terre cy énoncée afin qu'il en jouisse sans aucun empêchement quelconque. C'est pourquoy nous avons fait nos marques accoutumées

Je Soussigné Certifie que les chefs cy dessus ont fait leurs Marques, et donné Volontairement la terre cy dessus énoncée au Detroit le 28 Juillet 1780   Williams Juge apais

Enregistré au Greffe du Detroit en le registre No. 2 folio 27 par moy   Williams

45

Deed by Pottawattamie Chiefs to Pierre Labady.

Translated by Rudolph Worch & Dr. E. Krusty, Editors "Michigan Volks freund"

We, the chiefs of the Pouthewatamis Nation of the Detroit after having deliberated upon the state actual state of the lands which we leave uncultivated since long, with the advice and consent of and in the name of the entire nation, have determined to give a portion hereof to our friend Pierre Labady, containing three arpents front on the River Raisin at the right in ascending the said river and maintaining the same depth as the other lands heretofore given away up to a hundred arpents, adjacent to the said land on one side, down the river, is that of Mr Jean Baptiste Sanscrainte and on the other side up the river, that of the widow lady of Alexis Lampreau, and for the good friendship which we bear him, we light for him a fire of peace and tranquillity warranting to him from now and forever the said piece of land herein described that he may enjoy it without any hindrance whatever. For this purpose we have now our accustomed marks on the 15th of May 1786.

Kisinim   Windigo

Wawigattra

Achkybagoa   Ommouchkisis   Tchibinor

P. Sanscrainte

Fr. Navarre, Witnesses

46

now the state's borders. They belonged to six major tribes: Ottawa, Potawatomi, Miami, Chippewa — or Ojibway — Menominee and Wyandot.

Many place names, including "Michigan" itself, are of Native American origin, such as Kalkaska, Osceola, Washtenaw, Shiawassee, Cheboygan, Mackinac, Saginaw and Newaygo.

It was along the Grand River, in what is now Kent County's Ada Township, that a future chief of the Potawatomi's Forks Thornapple Band 1 was born in about 1800. The child's precise birthplace remains unknown because his tribe, like many others, lived in seasonal camps, moving around because the land belonged to all.

That infant named George Ne-be-nay-ge-zhick was destined to become a signer of treaties between area tribes and the federal government in distant Washington, D.C. He became a signatory of the 1836 treaty of the Ottawa, Chippewa and Potawatomi. In 1853, his name appears on the annuity roll of the Grand River Ottawas. And in 1856, he signed another treaty on behalf of the Ottawa and Chippewa. As a descendant put it, "The Indians had all that land but were snookered out of it by the government."

There was a clash of societies and values, with the settlers unable or unwilling to accept that the wilderness of the frontier was not really empty. As historian Bruce Catton explains:

> It was occupied by the Indians, who had been living there for a great many centuries, and by their standards it already held all the people it could support. The European of that day simply was not fitted to understand that the Indian actually was using this land. The Indian's towns were few, small and far apart; some of them were hardly more than temporary camps. But the very nature of the Indian's society meant that it needed vast tracts of untamed land. A settled, cultivated country was one in which the Indian culture could not survive.

47

Thus the snookering involved more than real estate. Expansion by white settlers came at the expense of heritage and the spirit of the land as the federal government forced many Native Americans from Michigan to move west of the Mississippi. Others were allowed to remain in Michigan but involuntarily moved to reservations.

One chief, Speckled Snake, expressed strong feelings about pressures from the white immigration in 1829, even before the massive relocations that were to come:

> Brothers! I have listened to many talks from our great father. When he first came over the wide waters, he was but a little man . . . very little. His legs were cramped by sitting long in his big boat. And he begged for a little land to light his fire on.
>
> But when the white man had warmed himself before the Indians' fire and filled himself with their hominy, he became very large. With a step he bestrode the mountains, and his feet covered the plains and the valleys. His hands grasped the eastern and western sea. And his head rested on the moon. Then he became our great father. He loved his red children, and he said, 'Get a little further, lest I tread on thee.'
>
> Brothers, I have listened to a great many talks from our great father. But they always began and ended in this—'Get a little further. You are too near to me.'

In 1830, Congress passed the Removal Act to compel mass relocation, an official policy that sometimes was reinforced through bribery and economic coercion.

In 1835, the Ottawa and Chippewa wrote to former territorial governor Lewis Cass, then U.S. Secretary of War, to say they were willing to sell some land but not to move: "It is a heartrending thought to our simple feelings to think of leaving our native country forever, the land where our forefathers lay thick in the earth." A few months later, the Ottawa of Grand Rapids wrote to President Andrew Jackson, saying, "You know we obtained our land from the Great Spirit. He made it for us who are

Indians. When we die, we expect to rest on this land. . . . We have not a mind to remove to a distant land."

Despite such pleas and protestations, many were removed, and the white settlers continued to flood the soon-to-be-state of Michigan.

In his memoirs, Indian agent, explorer and geologist Henry Rowe Schoolcraft later wrote angrily about the removal law, saying, "The whole Indian race is not, in the political scales, worth one white man's vote."

In addition to customs and laws and political traditions, a major long-lasting legacy brought from home by the settlers was the name chosen for their new community. Not surprisingly, New York is best-represented geographically on today's Michigan map as it was demographically by the immigrants more than a a century and a half ago. For example, Rochester, Mt. Morris, Bath, Utica, Albion, Ithaca, Troy, Batavia and Romulus all have antecedents in the Empire State.

That identity of names was neither whim nor coincidence. It reflect the wishes of many newcomers to maintain ties with their own roots. John Hanses and his companions from Germany undoubtedly felt psychological reassurance by giving their new Clinton County community the name of their distant hometown, Westphalia. Vermontville was named for the home state of its organizers, Dayton for the Ohio city where many of its pioneers came from, and Plymouth for the Massachusetts landing place of some local settlers' forebears.

When it came to naming the new capital city after statehood, the designation Michigan, Mich., was initially selected but dropped after a few months. Alternatives such as Pewanogawink, El Dorado and Swedenborg were considered and rejected before the city was finally named by Joseph H. North to honor his upstate New York home town of Lansing —which itself had been named after New York Revolutionary War hero John Lansing.

More important than counting heads or tracing places on a map were the pioneers themselves.

By definition, they were visionaries. Some yearned for a small farm of their own, for uncharted lakes and rivers to fish, for escape from predictability or financial distress, for political influence, for economic wealth, for independence from unwanted family ties, for untapped resources to profit from and sometimes exploit.

Often a combination of factors spurred them. For example, personal ambition and the realities of Scottish inheritance laws motivated John Millar to leave his native county. As the youngest son of a landed lord in Scotland, Millar could not directly inherit any of his father's land. Instead, he received a cash inheritance when his father died, then emigrated to the United States. Although he had studied medicine in Scotland, he worked as a construction overseer on the Erie Canal, then moved to Clinton Township, Macomb County, where he amassed 1,300 acres of fertile bottomland along the Clinton River.

In a tangible sense, dreaming came with the territory.

So it was with Michael Beach Jr., a War of 1812 veteran who arrived on the frontier and became an explorer, a wanderer and again a soldier. When Beach settled in Troy, he envisioned a canal between Lake Erie and Lake Michigan. It would be a "grand link in the chain of communication from the City of New York to the Mississippi," a way to lure "men of respectability to the frontier," in the words of a petition Beach and like-minded men sent to Congress. Although their vision of a canal failed to materialize, Michigan still grew.

Some people moved to Michigan almost precipitously, prompted by rumors and second-hand tales of opportunity. Others became familiar with Michigan through military service, commerce or exploratory trips they made before deciding whether to relocate their families.

That's what happened in 1701, when Francois Bienvenu dit

DeLisle, a French-born Quebecois, helped Antoine de la Mothe Cadillac establish Fort Pontchartrain as a French military outpost in what is now Detroit. A year later, DeLisle returned to Canada for his wife and baby. Connecticut-born Chauncey D. Wolcott did the same thing. Liking what he saw during a reconnaissance journey, Wolcott returned east for his family before opening a store in North Farmington.

While most settlers emigrated solo or just with their families, others combined forces back home to plan and carry out a joint trip and joint settlement. In 1827, for example, Capt. Gad Chamberlin, John B. Hollister and Erastus Day Sr. gathered in western New York to plan an expedition that would culminate in the establishment of a 32-member colony near Romeo. Their aim, one of Hollister's children wrote more than eight decades later, "was to give to each of their boys a farm and let them grow up with the country. As land could be had within five miles in any direction from their landing place at one dollar and a quarter an acre, such a purpose was within their means, as it could not have been at the East."

No common thread of education or skills united the new arrivals. Immigrants included the illiterate and the well-read, some masters of crafts, some with few practical abilities for survival.

Welcome Mathewson, a Rhode Islander who settled in Brownstown Township, Wayne County, apparently was unable to read or write. A grandson recalled him as an "uneducated man," and he signed all documents with an 'X.'

In contrast. some arrived already formally educated. There was John Reno, for example, who had been well-schooled in his native France, then prospered as a Detroit merchant. He became active in politics and civic affairs, and served as a state legislator and city assessor.

In terms of formal schooling, Roswell Burt of Davisburg, Oakland County, fell in between Mathewson and Reno and, thus, may have been more typical of Michigan settlers at the time of statehood: "I was born in Royalton, New York, December 31, 1821, brought to Michigan by my parents in 1826. Had the usual limited educational advantages of the sons of the pioneers; learned the trade of carpenter and joiner and also worked at wagon making." Those words come from an account Burt wrote late in life. The document was found in a steamer trunk several generations later by his descendants.

The Erie Canal made it easier to reach Michigan, but travel through the territory was often difficult. Many areas were not only roadless but even unexplored. The words "interminable swamp" were printed across the interior of Michigan on the map in a standard geography text for schoolchildren.

In addition, human conflicts and treachery arose — giving lie to the myth of total congeniality, camaraderie, good Samaritanism and openness on the frontier. That's what William Van Blarcom and his son Joseph painfully discovered along the Chicago Road near the border of Branch and Hillsdale counties. While the Van Blarcoms slept at an inn in 1835, thieves stole a strongbox strapped to their wagon. A search for the culprits failed, and "nothing resulted other than to swell their expenses at the house of the rascal who perpetrated the robbery himself," according to an account that blames the innkeeper for the theft.

Life was frequently difficult, even for those who would eventually prosper. Isaac Truax and his wife Angela DeLa Grange initially lived in a cave-like shanty built into the side of a hill when they settled in Oakland County. The family's only income was a $5-per-pelt bounty offered on wolves. For the family of Timothy Horace Ives and Sophia Hale, the first bitter Michigan winter near the St. Joseph River in Berrien County became even harsher when a local Potawatomi chief demanded gifts to allow them to remain on tribal land. The "gifts" turned out to be most of the food they had stored for the winter, so the Ives family made do with wild game and parched corn.

Pioneer home. Frontier housing generally began with the basics. Using an ax, saw and auger, settlers quickly erected a one-room log cabin because their highest priority was clearing land for crops, tilling new fields, planting seed and putting up fences and outbuildings for livestock rather than personal comfort. A.B. Copley, son of an early Van Buren County settler, wrote, "The houses were invariably log cabins, the logs notched on the under side with the saddle on top, and when additional room was required the double cabin plan was adopted, that is two cabins with the ends eight or 10 feet apart and the space roofed over, the cabin doors opening into the hall. The chimneys were built on the outside of one end, the jambs were made of clay pounded hard and the upper part of the chimney made of sticks daubed with clay." If the farm proved successful, a frame home was likely to follow. *State Archives of Michigan*

Farms were hacked out of the woods or perched on the prairies. Housing began with the fundamental need for quick shelter.

Other pioneers decided that the remoter regions of the territory were not for them but were unwilling to give up on Michigan altogether. The Canadian-born parents of John H. Carew were among those. They started in Monroe County but tired of the "hardships of their backwoods life" and moved to Ypsilanti and then Detroit, according to a family history. Carew discov-

53

Walker Tavern. The Walker Tavern (*opposite*) was a favorite stopping point for settlers and travelers in southern Michigan, located at the junction of the Chicago-Detroit and Jackson-Monroe roads in Lenawee County. Its guests included James Fenimore Cooper and Daniel Webster. The tavern is now part of Cambridge State Historic Park. *Michigan Bureau of History*

ered that commerce rather than agriculture ran in his blood, and he went into the masonry and wholesale and retail fruit and grocery businesses. He also opened a Detroit tea shop "familiarly known as the Yokohama," its wall painted like a Japanese garden.

It sometimes seemed prudent, if not essential, to reassure the folks back home that the journey to the frontier was safe. As Theodore Foster Talbot prepared to board an Ohio River ship in Indiana in April 1822, he wrote his wife in Kentucky: "Our steamboat is furnished with a low steam engine and the danger to be apprehended from bursting of course does not attach to this boat. I beg you to have no unusual anxiety about me."

The Dodge Tavern in Paw Paw was a favorite stopping spot on the Territorial Road from Detroit to St. Joseph. It was sometimes so crowded with weary pioneers that there were jokes about travelers who would offer a dollar "for a post to lean against." Another popular stopover was the Walker Tavern at the junction of the Chicago Road and the road between Jackson and Monroe.

Here's an uncomfortable travel reality that Joseph M. Griswold described about his family's 1836 trip from Toledo to Brooklyn, Jackson County: "I remember my father had to pay tribute to several proprietors of mud holes in the swampy country whose ox teams stood ready before their doors, and for a consideration would help the unfortunate movers past their possessions. How dreary was that slow journey through the low lands."

54

Thaddeus Smith. Thaddeus and Eliza Smith came from Virginia to Prairie Ronde, Kalamazoo County, in 1830. Their son Henry Parker Smith later remembered how the family made the "long, tiresome journey through swamps and dense forest" and were welcomed into the home of recent Ohio immigrant William Duncan. "Very soon after, we were gathered into the one square room of the house and I was allowed to absorb a bowl of bread and milk. Father and  Mother and the teamster also had their supper of corn bread and butter washed down with sage tea, which they ate with an appetite that everybody carried with them in those days of scanty fare and hardship." *State Archives of Michigan*

Once the rugged journeys were over, there still were hardships aplenty. Bad weather —summer drought, late spring and early fall frosts, flooding —took its toll on crops. Wild animals such as bears and wolves took their toll on precious livestock.

Virginian Thaddeus Smith confronted prairie wolves in isolated Kalamazoo County. His son Henry Parker Smith wrote of the "nightly serenades" of the wolves

who would gather about our doors and night hideous with their dismal howls and barks. We kept the chickens in a box in the house, otherwise they would be snatched up in short order by these hungry demons. These concerts were arranged upon a regular program. . . . As soon as it was dark and the lights were extinguished, some old veteran would open it with a solo in a minor key with very little variation, then another would join in, and another . . . with the chorus of from 35 to 50 voices.

Diseases such as cholera and consumption took a heavy human toll. In a letter to his New England in-laws, Jefferson Gage Thurber of Monroe wrote:

> In 1832, while the cholera was in Detroit, I was there during the whole of it. I was a daily attendant in the hospitals, both of the Army and of the citizens. From the fact of not having it, I concluded it was not contagious. The panic at that time exceeded anything I ever imagined. The timidity of our border settlers from sudden incursions of the Indians forms but a faint comparison. I have no doubt from what little experience and observation I have had that fear has killed as many as the cholera.

Of course, the settlers were not the only ones devastated by disease. A Saginaw County history relates the impact of small-pox in that area in the mid-1830s:

> The small-pox entered the Indian villages about this time, and added largely to increase the prevailing dread of some impending disaster. Providence, however, ruled that the pioneers might suffer alone from financial reverses, while the Indians would be carried away in thousands by the dreadful disease. Of the entire number of the doomed race then dwelling in the neighborhood of the Great Camp, over 2,000 perished, the remainder fled to the wilderness to seek a hiding place where the Great Spirit could not find them, or pursue them with his vengeance.

In his memoirs, Alden Giddings wrote about Oakland County: "While living in Independence, I have many times, while hunting cattle, passed over the cemetery where the Indian victims of smallpox were buried. It appears that years before, that disease nearly exterminated a tribe in that vicinity."

Challenging the frontier in groups rather than alone was no guarantee that things would go smoothly. Consider a woman who helped settle Clinton County's Duplain Township as part of a group of hometowners from the East. At one point, she

57

cried out despairingly to her husband, "Why have you brought us here in the wilderness to die?"

Some settlers arrived on the frontier with ample funds jingling in their pockets to start a new life. British-born Thomas Cade bought 400 acres of land when he settled in Sherman Township, St. Joseph County, and could afford to spend $100 in gold for a log house of "choice white oak timber."

By comparison, many others came with few material assets, among them Henry Caruss, who emigrated from New York to Commerce Township, Oakland County, "with his wife and three children and nothing else, except 25 cents after paying for his land, and commenced to hew out a living and a home amid the wilds of the then-unbroken forest," according to an historical account.

How tight was cash on the frontier? A 19th-century history of Oakland County put it this way:

> Many were often without even a cent of money, and, as a sample of the hard times, the fact may be stated that people were often without the necessary amount of funds to pay the postage on letters which came to them, and were obliged to work and earn it before they could get the letters from the office.

The price of postage for a one-ounce letter from the East was 25 cents, to be paid by the recipient rather than by the sender. And if three or four letters happened to arrive at the same time, "it is possible that the satisfaction of receiving news from friends may have been overbalanced by the regret caused at being obliged to pay so much postage."

Josiah Begole was among the settlers who started with few material assets. He arrived in Flint with $100 in his pocket but with an incalculable amount of energy and ambition in his soul. He taught school, bought farmland, acquired a sawmill and wagon-making business and parlayed political aspirations into a state Senate seat, a term in Congress and — after switching from

Henry and Temperence Bishop Caruss. Henry and Temperence
Caruss were typical of settlers who arrived on the frontier with little
money. They had only 25 cents left over after buying 160 acres of land
in Commerce Township, Oakland County. Their gamble and privation paid off with hard work, however. By the time Henery died in
1878, it could be said: "He lived to see all his children grown up into
useful, honored citizens, and well-settled in life, except the youngest
for whose support and education he made ample provision in his will."
Byron & Thelma Caruss

the Republicans to the Greenback Party —two years as
governor.

   Immigrants such as Begole shaped the highest echelons of
Michigan government well into the 20th century. Starting with
Virginia, where Stevens T. Mason was born, 12 other states,
Canada, England and Mexico have been the birthplaces of a

Begole tombstone. Josiah W. Begole had little money when he came to Michigan Territory but died wealthy after successful careers in farming, business and politics. The former governor is buried in his adopted community of Flint. *William Anderson, The Detroit News*

majority of governors. In fact, it wasn't until 1880 that a Michigan native was elected governor. That distinction went to David H. Jerome, the state's 17th governor, who was born in Detroit eight years before statehood. No Michigan-born successor would come again until the 29th governor, Alexander J. Groesbeck, took office in 1921.

Even by 1837 when statehood was achieved, Michigan was essentially a collection of small scattered communities, scattered farms and scattered wilderness outposts, with its approximately 175,000 non-Indians spread unevenly over 58,527 square miles. Detroit was the only city. Although it boasted a zoo and more than a dozen lawyers, its population was only 9,000.

Pioneers made marks of varying significance in their chosen land. The names of relatively few are remembered in state and national history. Others are now forgotten, with even the inscriptions on their tombstones eroded away by decades of tough Michigan weather.

Not all aspired to high office. Even the people who made the decisions and ran the government from the building that served first as territorial Capitol, then as state Capitol, did so only on a parttime basis.

More common were those who expressed community commitment and civic pride in more modest but equally important ways. Austin N. Kimmis Sr. was representative of them, a shoemaker-turned-farmer who served as Oakland County sheriff, deputy U.S. marshal, assistant assessor of internal revenue and longtime Novi Township supervisor. Pioneers like Kimmis organized local governments, served as tax collectors and township clerks, sat on school boards and city councils, or provided justice as sheriffs, judges, prosecutors and justices of the peace.

Others were satisfied with, or accepted, a quieter existence. As an Ionia County history observed of William C. Reed, "Save for the fact he was exceedingly poor, he was not conspicuous."

David H. Jerome. Born in Detroit in 1829, David Jerome was the first Michigan native to serve as governor. He led a peripatetic life: His father died while Jerome was an infant, so he went with his mother to New York for several years, then returned to Michigan where he was educated in St. Clair County. He later worked as a miner in California before coming to Saginaw, where he prospered as the owner of hardware and lumber businesses. He was a Civil War colonel, state senator  and member of the U.S. Board of Indian Commissioners before winning the governorship as a Republican in 1880. In office he advocated prudent government spending. After a narrow reelection defeat, Jerome moved back to New York, where he died. He is buried in Saginaw. *State Archives of Michigan*

Wanderlust made Michigan a way station rather than a permanent home for some. They may have been disillusioned with what they found in the territory, or homesick for what they left behind, or just too itchy, frightened, flighty or ambitious to stay long in any one place.

Albert and Mahlon Gore arrived in Calhoun County with their parents in 1836, boarded a train for Iowa in 1862, then helped South Dakota earn statehood. Albert later became a Missouri newspaper publisher, returned to Michigan for a while to farm and preach, then moved to California. Mahlon ended up as mayor of Orlando, Florida.

Similarly, Rufus Chancy Abbott and his wife Malvina Tillottson spent their lives together on the move from New York to

The Detroit waterfront at statehood. By 1837 and statehood, the one-time French military outpost of Fort Pontchartrain had become the bustling port of Detroit, with a theater, zoo and museum, along with taverns, hotels and more than a dozen lawyers. It was Michigan's only incorporated city at the time. *State Archives of Michigan*

Southfield to Allegan County to New York again to Pennsylvania to New York a third time and, finally, to Indiana. "I guess they were just restless," observed a descendant.

The pregnant and recently widowed Olive Selkrig Webb was merely passing through Detroit in 1836 on her way from New York to Niles when she gave birth to Sarah Lorrinilla Webb. The family remained in Michigan for only a few years, then went to St. Louis and on to Texas. Sarah Webb thrived in San Antonio —where she married a mayor-to-be and entertained such celebrities as Robert E. Lee, Ulysses S. Grant and Sam Houston —but some of her descendants returned to Michigan.

Hall & Mooney Lith. Buffalo

Territorial and State Capitol. Michigan's territorial Capitol in Detroit housed the state government in Detroit until 1847, when Lansing was designated as the capital city. The cornerstone was laid in 1823, construction was completed in 1828 and the building burned down in 1893. *Michigan Capitol Committee*

Rich or poor, literate or unlettered, interested in politics or not, religious or not, what enticed — or drove — the pioneers to Michigan?

On one level was the lure of rumor and hype.

A newspaper obituary of Leonard Keene Jr. related how, 48 years earlier, he and his wife Alice Shaffer had left their Ohio farm and "started for the great west and the Garden of Eden to be found in southwestern Michigan." The Keenes found their Eden in Cass County.

Similarly, in 1909, Dr. John H. Hollister, who had come to Macomb County as a child before statehood, recollected, "The territory of Michigan was then just being opened for settlement and was competing with Ohio as the El Dorado of the West, and the cry, 'Go west, young man' was heard long before Mr. (Horace) Greeley's time."

Not everybody envisioned Michigan as an Eden or an El Dorado, however. As one well-known poem put it, "Don't go to Michigan, that land of ills; the word means ague, fever and chills." And Edward Tiffin, a land surveyor, asserted that "not one acre in a hundred . . . would in any case admit of cultivation."

To help combat bad publicity about swamps and mosquitoes, active publicity and recruitment campaigns were developed to attract immigrants, as reflected in the song "Michigania," which was popular in the early 19th century:

> Come all ye Yankee farmers who wish to change your lot.
> Who've spunk enough to travel beyond your native spot.
> And leave behind the village where Pa and Ma must stay.
> Come follow me, and settle in Michigania.
>   Yea, yea, yea, in Michigania."

> Then there's old Varmount, well, what d'ye think of that?
> To be sure, the gals are handsome, and the cattle very fat.
> But who among the mountains, 'mid clouds and snow, would
>   stay.

TO EMIGRANTS.

At a respectable meeting of the citizens of

the vicinity of Mill-Creek, on the 19th inst. *Rufus Crossman* was called to the Chair, and *Samuel W. Dexter* chosen Secretary; the following resolutions were unanimously adopted.

1st—That we resolve ourselves into a society, to be called " *The Washtenaw County Society for the information of Emigrants ;*" and that the citizens of the county be requested, to unite with us for the purpose of advancing the objects of this society.

2d—There shall be a President, Vice-President, Corresponding Committee, Secretary of the Corresponding Committee, and Secretary of the society.

3d—That all meetings of the society shall be called by the president or vice-president, and notified by the secretary of the society.

4th—That it shall be the duty of the secretary of the corresponding committee, to correspond with all societies in any part of the United States, who may apply for information respecting the soil, climate, local advantages &c. of the territory of Michigan, and the inducements which any portion of the country offers to emigrants; and generally, to answer all questions, and supply all information upon the subject of emigrating to this territory.

5th—That it shall be the duty of the secretary of the corresponding committee, to prepare a brief description of the territory of Michigan, and of the local advantages of the different sections of the territory; together with an address to the citizens of the United States, who may be disposed to emigrate to this country, and to publish the same in one or more papers of the territory.

6th—That Gov. Cass, be the president of this society; that Silas Kingsley, be the vice-president; that Messrs. John Biddle, Jonathan Kearsley, John Mullett, Lucius Lyon, Sylvester Sibley, Orange Risdon, and Cyril Nichols, be members of the corresponding committee; that Samuel W. Dexter be secretary of the corresponding committee, and secretary of the society, *pro tem.*

7th—That the preceding resolutions be published in the Detroit papers, with a request to printers in different parts of the United States to republish the same; and that a certain number of handbills to the same effect be struck off, and distributed abroad; and that it be the duty of the secretary of the society to carry this resolution into effect.

R. CROSSMAN, Ch'n.
S. W. DEXTER, Sec'y.

Mill-Creek, Washtenaw County, Feb. 19, 1827.　　Sheldon & Wells, Printers—*Detroit, Mich. Ter.*

Soliciting settlers. The Washtenaw County Society for the Information of Emigrants (*opposite*) was formed to entice settlers to Michigan Territory and boost its population high enough to qualify for statehood. The group was organized in 1827 with territorial Gov. Lewis Cass as president. Other founders included John Biddle, the clerk of the U.S. Land Office in Detroit who would later become a territorial delegate to Congress, speaker of the state House of Representatives and mayor of Detroit; newspaper publisher Samuel Dexter; and Lucius Lyon, who was destined to be one of Michigan's first territorial U.S. senators. *State Archives of Michigan*

> When he can buy a prairie in Michigania?
>   Yea, yea, yea, in Michigania."

Another tune of the day was the "Emigrant Song," which boasted — with some exaggeration:

> Here is the place to live at ease,
> To work or play, just as you please;
> With little prudence any man
> Can soon get rich in Michigan.
> We here have soils of various kinds
> To suit men who have different minds,
> Prairies, openings, timbered land,
> And burr oak plains, in Michigan.

The Washtenaw County Society for the Information of Emigrants was founded in 1827. Its mission included correspondence with groups "in any part of the United States, who may apply for information respecting the soil, climate, local advantages &c of the territory of Michigan." In a newspaper ad published in Detroit for distribution across the country, the society pledged "to answer all questions, and supply all information upon the subject of emigrating to this territory."

And land speculators such as Lucius Lyon, who would later become a territorial U.S. senator, actively promoted the sale of

Dr. Douglass Houghton. Douglass Houghton (*opposite*), a versatile physician who had come from New York to Detroit in 1830 to lecture about geology and chemistry, became the first state geologist in 1837. Earlier, he had explored the northern reaches of the territory on two trips with Indian agent Henry Schoolcraft, finding copper traces on the Keweenaw Peninsula. As state geologist, he discovered the Saginaw Valley salt beds, and his 1841 report to the Legislature about copper in the Upper Peninsula triggered a mining rush. He was elected mayor of Detroit in 1842, and the first free public schools in the city opened during his tenure. He died in 1845 when his boat capsized in Lake Superior. A county, city and the state's largest inland lake are named for him. It was written of Houghton that he "liked the study of nature better than books." *State Archives of Michigan*

property they owned. In a broadside advertising "village lots at auction" in Ypsilanti, Lyon wrote:

> To those who are not acquainted with it . . ., situated as it is upon a navigable stream, and that one of the finest in the Territory, with the advantages of water power to any extent, surrounded by a pleasant, healthy and fertile country, and watered by numerous crystal springs of the clearest and purest water, with the great road from Detroit to Chicago passing directly through it, Ypsilanti cannot fail of becoming, at no very distant period, one of the most important towns in Michigan.

> The unexampled rapidity with which the county of Washtenaw has settled is evidence of the value of this section of country; and the local position of Ypsilanti, with its abundance of water power, render it one of the most eligible situations for a large manufacturing town, in the western country, where the enterprise of the capitalist, the mechanic and manufacturer will be sure to find a speedy reward.

There was puffery in some promotional claims and outright fraud in others. In 1837, explorers Douglass Houghton and Bela Hubbard looked for well-promoted White Rock City along the shores of Lake Huron. Wrote Hubbard: "Maps executed in the

Bela Hubbard, a wealthy Detroit property owner and civic activist, accompanied Douglass Houghton on geological explorations. On an 1837 survey expedition in the Thumb, the two men looked for the purported town of White Rock City on Lake Huron. Promoters of the community had distributed a detailed map showing a bustling harbor and busy sawmills, steamships on a wide river, churches and homes, a bank, wide streets and a city square. When Hubbard and Houghton arrived, they found no buildings, however. There was a narrow creek rather than a river, and three beech trees instead of a public square. Hubbard later said they became the first guests at the the White Rock City Hotel, having registered by carving their names into one of the beeches. *Michigan State University Archives & Historical Collections*

highest style of the typographer's art, displayed in hotel bar-rooms and other places, where congregate the thousand seekers after fortune that courted the happy possessor of valuable lots and water privileges —had announced its unrivalled situation and advantages. Auctioneers had sounded its praises and struck off its lots at fabulous prices to anxious buyers." So what did he and Houghton find? "Churches, houses, mills, people were all a myth. A thick wilderness covered the whole site."

New York-born Stephen Knapp negotiated to buy land in southern Michigan from a man identified as Edmund B. Brown. When Knapp returned to settle on his new property, he learned Brown had no title because it was owned by the government.

70

"This Brown was a land-shark and perpetrated his little joke on quite a number of settlers," according to one account.

Despite the puffery and despite the fraud, there was a solid basis for pioneer dreams. There was fertile farmland in parts of the territory, and timber to build the cities of the Midwest, and fish to feed the region's growing population, and water power for the mills and factories that would come. Explorers such as Houghton, the first state geologist, and his associate Hubbard disclosed the presence of natural resources galore, such as the copper of the Upper Peninsula and the salt beds of the Saginaw Valley.

Did the pioneers make the right decision coming here?

While most appeared satisfied, for others the experience fell short of expectations, of dreams, of needs. Some of the disgruntled headed back east or further west, or remained unhappily where they were. Hillsdale College archivist and historian Jerome A. Fallon explained why many of those who failed to do well in Michigan refused to return home: "They didn't want to admit they hadn't found the pot of gold at the end of the rainbow. It would have been an admission of defeat, so they lived under the most primitive conditions."

Still, there was more behind the flood of pioneers than mere hip-hip-hooray or promises of a pot of gold —generally in the form of rich soil — at the end of the rainbow. Travel was arduous in those days, and such a move frequently meant that the pioneers would never again see the parents, grandparents, siblings and friends who stayed behind.

As one woman put it at the 1905 meeting of the Michigan Pioneer and Historical Society, "Would our daughters of today meet the difficulties, perplexities and terrors with as much grace and endurance as did their grandmothers and great grandmothers in the pioneer days of Michigan?" The same question could be asked now about our sons and daughters.

The frontier meant sacrifices, even for those with money and health and stamina.

All were tested. Some succeeded. Others failed. All tried.

Francis Bienvenu dit DeLisle and Geneveva Charon dit LaFerriere

A builder of Fort Ponchartrain

As a soldier, Francis Bienvenu dit DeLisle helped lay out Fort Ponchartrain, the future Detroit. Here the French hoped to offset the power of the British, ensconced farther north at Fort Michilmackinac guarding the vital Straits of Mackinac linking lakes Michigan and Huron.

Francis had been born in France in 1663, then moved to Quebec where he married Geneveva Charon dit LaFerriere. In 1701 he set out with explorer Antoine de la Mothe Cadillac to establish the fortress, stockade and trading post that would later become the city of Detroit.

What was living like for DeLisle and his colleagues in those early days? Historian Clarence M. Burton wrote: "The houses of the first comers were very small and very crude. They were covered with skins, or with split rails, and then with grass or straw. There were no floors, except the earth beaten hard by many footsteps. The window openings were covered with the

Antoine de la Mothe Cadillac came to North America in 1683 and was the military commander who established a strategic French outpost on the Detroit River in 1701. Francis DeLisle was among the 50 soldiers and 50 workers under his command at Fort Pontchartrain, the first white settlers in what is now the city of Detroit. A former privateer who prospered from the fur trade, Cadillac had a confrontational and arrogant personality that contributed to his frequent disputes with the Jesuit missionaries in New France and with the Company of the Colony of Canada. In a letter, Count Jerome de Pontchartrain, his patron in France and a minister to King Louis XIV, wrote, "Nobody can find any objection to the profits which you have made or will make at Detroit, as

long as you are using only just and legal means. I must say, however, that you show too much greed and that you should use more moderation. This will always make us fear to give you too much power." In 1711, he was appointed governor of Louisiana, where he remained until his 1716 return to France. This statue stands on the Detroit campus of Wayne State University. *Patricia Clay, Wayne State University*

skin of some animal. The only large buildings in the place were the warehouse and church, and here all the assemblies were held for entertainments."

74

Fort Ponchartrain. This drawing depicts Fort Ponchartrain, Detroit, in about 1740, a decade before Francis DeLisle's death. *State Archives of Michigan*

In 1702, the wives of Cadillac and Capt. Alphonse de Tonty became the first white women at the fort. That same year, Francis returned with some companions and a load of beaver pelts to Montreal to retrieve Geneveva and to discover that a son, Alexis, had been born in his absence.

Although the records of the earliest French settlement in Detroit were lost in 1703 when St. Anne's Church was

Madame Marie-Therese Cadillac arrives in Detroit. The wives of Antoine de la Mothe Cadillac and his second-in-command, Alphonse de Tonty, arrived by canoe at Fort Ponchartrain from Canada in 1702 to demonstrate France's intent to remain in Detroit. With them was the Cadillacs' son Antoine. Francis DeLisle's wife and son came later that same year. Friends of Cadillac's wife Marie-Therese Guton had attempted to talk her out of the trip, but she responded, "Do not waste your pity on me. I know the hardships, the perils of the journey, the isolation of the life to which I am going, yet I am eager to go." *Robert Thom under commission from Michigan Bell*

destroyed by fire, the family is believed to have worshipped in the primitive log cabin that served as the community's first Roman Catholic church.

Cadillac awarded Francis and Geneveva a home site on St. Louis Street. After Geneveva died, Francis married Mary Ann Lemoin in 1708. "It was the custom to grant residents of the fort a plot of land outside the walls for farming. They would work

Peter DeLisle, a great-great-great-grandson of original Detroit settlers Francis and Geneveva DeLisle, worked as a schoolteacher and grocer, among other occupations, and served as Springwells Township supervisor and justice of the peace before winning a seat in the Michigan House of Repre-sentatives as a Democrat. He (*opposite*) campaigned in favor of low taxes, home rule for local governments and penalties for election fraud. A newspaper report of his victory said he "let his antagonist do most of the work and the greater part of the talking, but when he did go out he 'sawed wood' every moment of the time," winning by 131 votes. As he once said, "That I served you honestly, a vote from you will show it. If I have not done my duty as a public officer, vote against." *William A. McQueen*

their land during the day and return to their home in the fort at night, Francis was granted strip farm number 15. Fruit trees were planted and the area was known for the pear trees that provided an abundant crop," descendant William A. McQueen wrote.

Detroit was slow to grow in those early years. By 1750, the year before Francis DeLisle's death, there were only 93 families living in the city. According to McQueen, "The church was the center of social activities. There was little time or reason for political concerns. The community held together working hard to provide the necessities of life."

Son Alexis initially helped on his parents' farm, but later was granted his own strip farm near the Rouge River, paying a percentage — determined by the commandant of the fort — of his crops as rent.

One descendant, Welcome DeLisle, provided the timber to build Fort Wayne to help protect Detroit from Canada after the War of 1812. He was politically active in Ecorse politics, serving as township treasurer, school inspector and highway commissioner. His son Peter served in the state Legislature.

Cobmosa

The last of our people
who could communicate with
the animals directly

Legends about Cobmosa, the Ottawa chief known as the "Great Walker," live on.

One tale tells how he fought a powerful "medicine bear" from Petoskey to Grand Rapids.

And witnesses claimed that Cobmosa could be at far-apart locations in the northern parts of the Lower Peninsula on the same day.

"My grandfather said he was the last of our people, of our family, who could communicate with the animals directly," recalled John V. Bailey, Cobmosa's great-great-great-great grandson. "He had great power. He had the power of goodness. He covered so much territory physically and mentally."

It was sometime in the mid-1700s — one historic marker puts it in 1768 — that Cobmosa was born near the junction of the Grand and Flat Rivers in what is now Lowell, Kent County. His

Indian schools. When Cobmosa's band and other Indians were forced by the federal government to move to an Oceana County reservation in 1858, four schools were built there for their children. One was named Cob-moo-sa after the chief and resembled this nearby Pay-baw-me School. Rev. D. R. Latham was the first teacher at the Cob-moo-sa School. *Oceana County Pioneers & Business Men of Today, 1890*

grandfather had come to the area in the 1600s from what became Harbor Springs.

It is known that Cobmosa — also called Cob-moo-sa — was displaced in 1833 when a group of white settlers arrived at what would become the city of Ionia and selected land occupied by his village. He moved to the bend of a nearby creek.

"He was chief speaker of his band, and in that respect was a wonder. I have never seen or heard his equal, and he had a great influence over the Indians of the Grand River valley," recalled J.S. Hooker, who knew Cobmosa in those days.

Another settler, Henry Sessions, told about Cobmosa's frequent visits with his father Alonzo Sessions, a future lieutenant governor: "I recollect father trading to him wheat for a double-barreled shotgun, with which I used to hunt turkeys and other game."

His name appears in an 1836 treaty that the federal government negotiated with the Chippewa and Ottawa tribes. Under that treaty ceding tribal lands, Cobmosa — identified as "Cawpemossay or the Walker" — was listed among the "chiefs of the first class" entitled to $500 each. He also signed an 1855 treaty in Detroit.

Then came 1858 when Cobmosa's Flat River Band and other tribes were forcibly relocated to a reservation in Elbridge Township, Oceana County. At that time, he told Indian commissioner William A. Richmond how his father had "espoused the cause of the American colonist in the War of Revolution and remained faithful to the end."

When the Civil War broke out, he gave a recruitment speech there on behalf of the all-Indian Company K of the 1st Michigan Sharpshooters.

Cobmosa was found dead in a canoe on or near his farm in 1866 at age 98 after a lifetime of prominence, remembered as a leader with "much dignity and manliness." He was buried at the Indian Cemetery in Elbridge Township because, as Bailey put it, the local clergy "refused to let a 'pagan' be buried in a Christian cemetery."

His tombstone no longer stands, and the cemetery, which was later sold to a farmer for cattle grazing, is no longer marked.

But the disappearance of physical symbols such as a gravestone or cemetery does not undermine the significance of the Great Walker's achievements because his influence far surpassed his physical capabilities.

1st Michigan Sharpshooters. After the Civil War erupted, Cobmosa gave a recruitment speech on behalf of the all-Indian Company K of the 1st Michigan Sharpshooters. Members of Company K were among more than 90,000 Michigan soldiers in the Union Army. Only one member of Company K was illiterate, contrasted with an illiteracy rate averaging 20 percent among the all-white companies of the 1st Michigan Sharpshooters. The regiment was organized during the winter of 1862–1863 in Kalamazoo, fought in 21 battles including Spottsylvania, Wilderness, Petersburg and Cold Harbor, and disbanded in Jackson in 1865. In addition to the 1st Michigan Sharpshooters, the state fielded 30 regiments of infantry, 11 of calvary, one of artillery and one of engineers. This statue (*opposite*) honoring the 1st Michigan Sharpshooters stands on the east lawn of the Capitol in Lansing. *Michigan Travel Commission*

George Meldrum and Angelique Mary Catherine Chapoton

Both adversity and prosperity

While many other Michigan pioneers were carving farms out of wilderness, George Meldrum opted for urban life.

Born in Scotland in 1737, Meldrum emigrated to North America and traveled to Detroit, where he was to encounter both adversity and prosperity as a merchant.

By the time he arrived, Michigan already had switched from French to British status, but the influence of colonists from France remained strong.

There he wed Angelique Mary Catherine Chapoton. Her French-born grandfather, John Chapoton, had been the first surgeon assigned to Fort Ponchartrain and served as medical practitioner for both the military garrison and local inhabitants.

Records show George was an active trader who provided goods to the British at Fort Michilmackinac under instructions from the colonial lieutenant governor, Patrick Sinclair. His mer-

Lieutenant Govenor Patrick Sinclair. As a trader in colonial Michigan, George Meldrum dealt with British Lt. Gov. Patrick Sinclair, shown in this silhouette, in providing goods to Fort Michilmackinac. From 1779 to 1781 during the American Revolution, Sinclair moved the British fort from Mackinaw City on the mainland to a Mackinac Island hilltop to avoid a potential attack by American troops under Col. George Rogers. The attack never materialized. *Mackinac Island State Park Commission, At the Crossroads, D. R. Atkins*

chandise included corn, canoes, brass knobs, fishing lines and spears, cloth, thread, grease and chisels.

Back in the Detroit area, George owned a number of parcels of real estate, including land on the Detroit River near Merchant's Wharf and property in what are now Hamtramck and

Reverend Gabriel Richard unsuccessfully negotiated to buy land for church use from George Meldrum in Detroit. A colorful personality, Richard once was jailed for three weeks for refusing to pay a $1,116 court judgment in a civil suit by an excommunicated former parishioner. It was Richard who opened schools in Detroit, issued the first newspaper west of the Allegheny Mountains and later served as territorial delegate to Congress for one term. In Washington, he regaled President James Monroe and Secretary of State John Calhoun with tales about his missionary work among northern Michigan tribes. In Congress, he helped win appropriations to open the Fort Gratiot, Pontiac, Grand River and Chicago roads, and donated his government salary to St. Anne's Church in Detroit. He lost reelection to Congress by only three votes. Later, he helped organize Michigan's first historical society and died in 1832 while tending victims of a cholera plague. *State Archives of Michigan*

Macomb County's Chesterfield Township. At one point, Father Gabriel Richard, Detroit's renowned priest and community leader, inquired about buying a lot for church use but no deal occurred.

Although George had been among those who elected Phillip Dejean as the first local judge in 1768, he incurred Dejean's wrath six years later. Details of the affront are lost to history, but published proceedings of the Detroit Land Board quote his public apology to the judge:

"Sir, I confess I have used you to very ill in the presence of the committee and several other merchants . . . by several rash and

Detroit fire of 1805. Tradition has it that the great fire of June 11, 1805, began when burning tobacco fell from a pipe —possibly that of baker John Harvey, possibly that of a stablehand —and ignited a pile of hay on a windy day. As George B. Catlin wrote in his history of the city: "The alarm quickly spread and soon every man in the village was rushing to the scene. . . . When night fell there was but one unimportant warehouse and a few tottering stone chimneys left standing above the glowing embers of what had once been the incorporated town of Detroit. All the labor and love and hope that had gone into the making of old Detroit were gone, without leaving a trace behind." George Meldrum's business, the merchant firm of Meldrum & Park, was among the buildings destroyed. *Robert Thom under commission from Michigan Bell*

unbecoming aspersions for which I am very sorry, and which I hope you will be so good as to forgive, as it was entirely the effect of liquor, whereof I had drank too freely."

Dejean had run-ins with other early Detroiters as well, history shows. One critical account described him as an unsuccessful merchant who was "short, fat and swarthy, of active mercurial temperment, with an exaggerated idea of his own importance, with a fixed conviction that his official dignity must be upheld at all hazards, a pompous pious bungler who was willing to send any suspect to the gallows on short notice for the fee there was in it." Some violators were ordered "to hoe in the judicial garden and replenish the judicial woodpile," another critic wrote. In 1778, a grand jury in Montreal charged Dejean with "unjust and illegal, tyrannical and felonious acts contrary to good government."

Despite —or perhaps because of —his conflict with Dejean, George Meldrum was in the good graces of the powers-that-be. The British colonial governor later appointed him as a district commissioner. He also won election as a trustee of Detroit when it was organized as a township.

He was a partner with William Park in the merchant firm of Meldrum & Park and suffered heavy losses when fire destroyed the entire city in 1805. He sold some of his real estate to help rebuild the city after the fire.

Shortly before his death, he was summoned to jury duty in a riot trial but was deemed too infirm to serve.

William McGulpin and Madeleine Bourassa

Mackinac Island legacy

For decades, one of the McGulpin family's physical legacies to Michigan lay disguised on Mackinac Island.

Now known as the McGulpin House, it was a small log cabin constructed in French-Canadian architectural style. Built with squared hand-hewn logs and hand-cut roof boards during British occupation of the island, it is believed to be one of the oldest buildings still standing in the old Northwest Territory.

One unverified theory is that it served as the original priest's house for the landmark St. Anne's Roman Catholic Church.

William bought the house in 1817. Subsequent owners altered and expanded it until the original structure could not be seen. Not until the early 1970s was the hidden architectural treasure discovered on a back street of the resort village.

The Mackinac Island State Park Commission acquired the building in 1982, moved it to historic Market Street and

McGulpin House. The Mackinac Island log house William McGulpin purchased in 1817 is among the oldest remaining buildings in what was the vast Northwest Territory covering the upper Midwest. It has been moved from its original location, restored to the style of the time when the McGulpins lived there, and is now open to visitors. *Mackinac State Historic Parks*

Mackinac Island 1813. This 1813 etching shows Mackinac Island as it appeared when William and Madeleine McGulpin lived there. A two-masted schooner is docked offshore and a large Indian birch bark canoe is on the beach near a row of traders' homes. Fort Mackinac, built by the British in 1779–1781, can be seen atop the hill. *State Archives of Michigan*

Furs, trappers & traders. As a baker, William McGulpin furnished bread to the American Fur Co., which John Jacob Astor organized in 1808 on Mackinac Island. This painting shows the company headquarters that served as the summer rendezvous point for hundreds of white and Native American traders and trappers. After the War of 1812, Congress limited the fur trade to American citizens, allowing Astor to buy out his Canadian competitors and develop a virtual monopoly on the fur trade in Michigan for 17 years. *Robert Thom under commission from Michigan Bell*

restored it to its 1820s appearance. The McGulpin House is now a popular stopping point on Mackinac Island tours.

William's father Patrick had emigrated from Scotland to Canada and headed for Detroit in 1776. There he worked as a tailor and soldier, and a few years later married Madeleine Crequi. William was born in Detroit in 1791.

The family eventually looked northward for its future, on the mainland of northern Michigan as well as on Mackinac Island, where William married Madeleine Bourassa.

In 1808, a claim was filed in the Detroit land office for 640 acres of land in Old Michilmackinac, just west of Mackinaw City. The family also purchased land in St. Ignace, north of the Straits.

William became a baker who furnished bread to the American Fur Co. and to the U.S. Army on the island.

The family name remains immortalized, not only in the cabin-turned-tourist-attraction but also on the tip of the Lower Peninsula where McGulpin's Point Lighthouse was built in the mid-19th century. The lighthouse remained in service until 1906 and is now a private home.

Shawano

Let a man run that can run.

Shawano. Born in one age. Died in a different world.

No government records note when the chief of the Chippewa Shawano band, whose name he carried, was born. No document identifies the name of his wife. And no stone marks his grave at the Bai de Wasai cemetery on Sugar Island near Sault Ste. Marie.

Even without the reams of paper that trail contemporary Americans through their lives, it is evident that Shawano played a significant role in Michigan's pre-statehood history.

The first official documentation of that role came in an 1820 treaty in which the Ottawa and Chippewa tribes ceded the St. Martin Islands in Lake Huron to the U.S. government in exchange for a quantity of goods. Shawano affixed his mark to the treaty at Michilmackinac, now known as Mackinac Island, along with territorial Gov. Lewis Cass, who would later serve in the Cabinet and U.S. Senate in Washington. It is likely that he also knew Henry Rowe Schoolcraft, the renowned Indian agent for the territory who was based in Sault Ste. Marie.

Yvonne Marie Peer, Shawano's great-great-great-great granddaughter, recalls a legend about how fast a runner Shawano was: According to tradition, Shawano passed a fox that was chasing a jackrabbit, then sped past the rabbit, saying, "Let a man run that can run."

He is identified by the name Kewayzi Shawano as a chief entitled to a $500 payment under an 1836 treaty that reserved Sugar Island and its islets as a tribal reservation. Sugar Island — originally Sisibakwato-miniss, or Maple Sugar — is the third-largest island in the St. Marys River.

Then an 1855 treaty gave to "O'Shaw-waw-no" a small cedar-and-balsam-covered island where he lived at the foot of the rapids on the St. Marys. Called Chief's or Oshawano's Island, it was located "in the swirl and foam of the falls" and was compared by visitors to "an emerald in a setting of white." He kept a birch bark canoe to travel back and forth to the mainland. In his later years, Shawano was described as "a chief without a nation, without a country." It was observed that "his manner was courtly, his speech grave and dignified with a tinge of sadness."

An Upper Peninsula history tells how Shawano's son Edward Oshawano attended school in Detroit and at Albion College, then studied law until somebody bit off his nose. The injury came in a fight that erupted during a card game aboard an ice-locked steamer in the St. Marys. Afterward, Edward eked out a living by fishing and hunting and "lived almost the life of a hermit, his place of residence alternating, as the fancy seized him, between the island of his name at the foot of the rapids and Sugar Island."

As for Shawano himself, the once-vigorous chief went blind in his older years and became upset when he realized that he had ceded his land to the government.

A Lower Peninsula county was called "Shawono" in his

Edward Oshawano and Cobogam. Chief Shawano's son Edward Oshawano, identified as Edward Shaw-waw-naw in the caption of this picture, is seated at the bottom left. Seated next to him is his brother Charles Kaw-baw-gam, also known as Cobogam or Chief Marquette. Shawano's third son Louis also served as a chief but is not pictured. On the far right of the bottom row is John Gurnoe, a friend of Indian agent and author Henry Schoolcraft. Gurnoe "carried the mail from the Sag to the Soo, worked on the old state locks and was superintendent of the county Poor Farm for 12 years," according to an Upper Peninsula history. Standing are John Boucher (left) and Louis Cadotte (right). "Each of these five men," the book said, "was noted for his good influences over the people from whom he descended, and his teachings by means of moral suasion and precept were of great and lasting value to the community." *Preston Hogue*

honor in 1840, but the Legislature changed its name to Crawford County three years later. And like Shawano the chief and Shawono the county, the island that carried his name also is no more: It disappeared during construction of the third Soo lock.

Joseph Loranger and Rosalie Chabert

Fled to safety and to war

There is no Euphonia, Mich., but if James Monroe hadn't made a presidential campaign stop in Detroit, the city of Monroe might now carry that name.

When fur trader Joseph Loranger platted his land in 1817 in what is now Monroe, he intended to name the new village after his farm "Euphonia." He even provided the land to be used for the county "court-house and gaol," or jail.

At the time he arrived, the community in the southeast corner of Michigan was known as Frenchtown. Then history — in the form of Monroe's visit — intervened and the community in 1824 was renamed instead for the fifth U.S. president.

Loranger, who had been born in Quebec, divided his time between the growing city of Detroit and the wilderness area of Monroe.

His wife Rosalie Chabert was a native Detroiter. When she was a child, her father Charles Francois Chabert de Joncaire

Joseph Loranger Sr. Canadian-born Joseph Loranger Sr. operated a successful trading post in Monroe and was a prosperous landowner in Detroit. At the time of his death in 1862, Joseph Sr.'s estate was valued at $100,000, a considerable sum for the times. *Monroe County Historical Commission*

Rosalie Chabert Loranger was the daughter of a politically influential Detroit delegate to the Northwest Territory General Assembly. *Monroe County Historical Commission*

served as one of the city's three delegates to the Northwest Territory's General Assembly in Cincinnati.

In Michigan's territorial days, Joseph and Rosalie experienced war and the kidnapping of their infant son.

Joseph Sr. was operating a trading post next to the River Raisin in Monroe when the War of 1812 broke out. The store was "stripped of all supplies" by a Potawatomi raiding party allied with the British, but an advance warning provided enough time for Joseph to flee across the river to safety. He then enlisted in the American struggle against the British.

In a separate incident, the couple's year-old son, Joseph Jr., was kidnapped from his cradle by a "renegade Indian," then was "carried off to wilderness near Ecorse," one account relates. Whiskey and trinkets were paid as ransom, and the child was returned unharmed after two days.

The fur trade proved extremely profitable, and the elder Loranger was able to afford to donate four parcels of land for public use in Monroe.

In Detroit, the family homestead was near the present site of the Ambassador Bridge. Records indicate that the elder Joseph owned four miles of land along the Detroit River and that as many as 50,000 whitefish could be caught off shore in a single night, earning $3 to $4 per hundred. His father-in-law's adjacent property stretched south along the river to Ecorse.

Michael Beach Jr. and Lucy Davis

The archetypal pioneer,
a sense of restlessness

Michael Beach Jr. was a soldier, a wanderer, a land trader, an explorer — and a dreamer.

One of those dreams? A canal across southern Michigan connecting Lake Erie to Lake Michigan.

It would be a "grand link in the chain of inland communication from the city of New York to the Mississippi," a way to entice "men of respectability to the frontier" and give Michigan a "dense population," according to a petition Beach and like-minded men sent to Congress. As for the proposed route across southern Michigan, they assured Congress, "there are no serious natural obstacles, there is but little rock, the land is easily excavated and sufficiently level without a serious hill."

That was in 1827, eight years after Beach emigrated from New York State to what is now Troy. He is believed to have been the first white settler in the area.

Beach homestead. Michael and Lucy Beach built this house on their Highland Township farm. It was destroyed by fire in 1891 when their 17-year-old grandson ignored warnings against burning leaves and brush in the yard. Live ashes ignited the wooden shingle roof, and the house burned to the ground. *Eugene H. Beach Jr.*

The canal was never dug, but even without it Michigan grew toward statehood.

"He was the archetypal pioneer. There is a sense of restlessness I detect there," said great-great grandson Eugene H. Beach Jr. "When he left western New York, that was still, by our standards, wilderness. Yet he left that for the even greater wilderness of Michigan." His ancestor, he said, was able to "successfully complete the transition from patriot and pioneer to settler and successful farmer; to pass from a life of risk and adventure to one of relative security and peace."

How was that transition made?

During the War of 1812, Michael served in the New York

Davis and Susan Jane (Jennie) Beach. Born two years before statehood, Davis Beach was one of nine sons of Michael and Lucy Beach. While five of his brothers headed for California during the Gold Rush, Davis stayed home to tend the farm and take care of his mother, his youngest brother and three younger sisters. He met his wife, Indiana-born Susan Jane (Jennie) Thomas, while she was visiting relatives in Michigan. *Eugene H. Beach Jr.*

militia. He then headed west to Detroit with fellow veteran Peter Van Avery, knapsacks on their backs. Van Avery later settled in the village of Franklin.

In 1821, Michael joined a survey party to explore and map new townships in Genesee County and the Saginaw River basin. He later served as a grand juror and testified as a defense witness at the first murder trial held in the county, that of a Bloomfield Township man acquitted on the basis of insanity of murdering his brother.

In 1829, he and his brother-in-law, Joshua Davis, opened the first sawmill in Southfield Township, on the east branch of the Rouge River.

Family tradition holds that Michael was among the more than 200 Michigan militia who served during the 1831–1832 Black Hawk War. It was about 1833 when Michael made his final move to a farmstead in Highland Township. Lanes of maples were planted in the yard, giving the farm the name of Maple Grove.

Michael died in Highland in 1855 and is buried alongside his wife of 33 years, Lucy Davis.

The family's quest for adventure didn't begin — or end — with Michael. His forebearers had come from England to Connecticut in 1639 and his father served in the Revolutionary War, then became an early settler of upstate New York.

Michael fathered 14 children, five of whom felt the wanderlust and joined the '49ers in the California gold rush. Only three survived that experience. A son also named Michael died there "of the privations encountered" and Horace was killed when "his claim was jumped by outlaws." Another son, Benjamin, was luckier — he became "involved in a disputed claim, and in order to escape with his life and his gold, he was packed in a shipping box and sent back east," a township history records.

Bela Chapman and Mary Charette

Trader, explorer, politician, judge

Even with powerful political enemies, Bela Chapman repeatedly won the confidence of his fellow northern Michiganians.

Running for the 1835 constitutional convention, the New Hampshire-born Chapman defeated the interests of Henry and James Schoolcraft, two Democratic powerhouses in the territory.

Henry was a noted explorer and expert on Michigan tribes who sat on the Territorial Council before statehood. Brother James later served in the Legislature.

In a March 14 letter to Henry, James wrote, "I have hard times in reference to the election for delegate to the convention, being that I have to contend against the whole village who are in favor of B. Chapman. To me, this election is of importance, as it will determine the political character of Michigan."

When the returns came in, Bela, a Whig, had won the contest

Old Mackinac Island courthouse. Bela Hubbard served as probate judge in this courthouse for four terms: 1840–1844, 1848–1853, 1860–1865 and 1866–1873. Although the county seat was moved to St. Ignace on the mainland in 1881 after his death, this building is still used as the Mackinac Island City Hall and police headquarters. *Eric Freedman*

Henry Rowe Schoolcraft was a major political rival of Bela Chapman. A geologist and explorer for whom Schoolcraft County and the village of Schoolcraft are named, he served as the mediator and treaty negotiator between the federal government and Michigan's Native Americans, a member of the Territorial Council and a University of Michigan regent. As a participant in the 1820 exploration of Michigan natural resources led by territorial Gov. Lewis Cass, he had confirmed the existence of the huge Ontonagon Copper boulder in the western Upper Peninsula. He remains well known for his writings about Indian ethnology, including books on tribal history and legends. Poet Henry Wadsworth Longfellow used some of the legends he collected as a basis for "The Song of Hiawatha." *State Archives of Michigan*

by two votes and was sent to Detroit as the Chippewa County representative to help draft Michigan's first constitution.

In a bitter post-election letter to Henry, James complained of irregularities, asserting that "men were forced to vote against their wills. . . . Lies, barefaced lies, were told to influence the ignorant. . . . It was not conducted by a political principle."

Census records show that Bela settled in Michigan sometime before 1820 and lived in Sault Ste. Marie and on Mackinac Island. A fur trader for the Astor Fur Co., he traveled widely through the Great Lakes region and kept a log of his journeys. He also spent one season as a sutler providing supplies to the Army at Green Bay, Wisc. As a government-authorized sutler, he wrote to Henry Schoolcraft in 1831 —several years before their political conflict —to complain that unlicensed sutlers operating in the area were hurting his business. Henry at the time belonged to the territory's Legislative Council in Detroit.

On his travels, Bela met and married Mary Charette in Fond du Lac, Wisc. Her mother Equameeg was a Chippewa, and her father Simon Charette was a renowned French-Canadian fur trader.

An 1826 treaty with the Chippewa tribe had awarded Mary 640 acres of land, but the government failed to honor that commitment. However, she later received 80 acres south of Cheboygan under an 1842 treaty.

After statehood, Bela served as Mackinac County probate judge, village president and delegate to the 1867 constitutional convention in Lansing.

Bela outlived his rivals, the Schoolcraft brothers, and continued to hold court on Mackinac Island until his death in 1873. Although the county seat was moved to St. Ignace on the mainland in 1881, the courthouse where he served is still used as the Mackinac Island City Hall and police headquarters.

Elizur Goodrich and Lucy Smith Fish

Wanderlust and public service

By the time statehood arrived in 1837, three generations of the Goodrich family were calling Michigan home.

It all started with Elizur Goodrich, a War of 1812 veteran who had been wounded in the Battle of Chippewa. Bereaved by the death of his first wife Lydia in 1822, he set off for a look at Michigan Territory.

Liking what he found, the Connecticut-born New Yorker decided to make a fresh start on the frontier with his seven sons.

Six of the boys sailed with Elizur aboard the schooner *Hannah* from Buffalo to Detroit, while the seventh drove the family's team overland through Canada. From Detroit, the road northward to Troy was terrible, "an empty lumber wagon being a load for a team," son Ira later recalled.

After settling in Oakland County, Elizur married the widow Lucy Smith Fish and, with his son Alanson, helped lay out the

Egbertson Goodrich. Sarah and Elizur Goodrich's son Egbertson tried his hand at lumbering in Newaygo County and farming in Clinton County before settling in Gratiot County. He was described as the "son of a pioneer who shared with his family the privations and pleasures of that variety of existence." *Portrait & Biographical Album of Gratiot County, 1884*

city of Auburn Hills. He purchased and operated a sawmill there as well. Elizur became Oakland County's first road commissioner and a trustee of Auburn Academy.

A county history tells about the first store in Auburn, which was owned by Zolman Carver. One of Carver's first transactions involved the Goodrich boys, who sold him 40 raccoon skins at 25 cents each. Carver resold them at 18 ³/₄ cents each and "charged the difference to profit and loss, and went out of business for a while."

Wanderlust struck Alanson, just as it had his father before him. After holding local office in Oakland County, Alanson moved to DeWitt, north of where Lansing would later be built. There he and his wife Sarah Stout donated land for the first public school in Clinton County. The log schoolhouse opened on their homestead in 1836, and children who lived too far away to walk were boarded at local homes.

Their son Egbertson also felt the itch to wander. He moved northwest to Newaygo County to try his hand at lumbering along the Muskegon River. He spent 10 years there before returning to DeWitt in 1860 and, five years later, bought 144 acres in Gratiot County between Alma and St. Louis.

Daniel Thompson and Susan Ann Bradley

Performed his duties to the entire satisfaction of all parties

Daniel Thompson had powerful friends, including President Andrew Jackson and Michigan's first governor, Stevens T. Mason.

The Connecticut native, who eventually would become sheriff of Wayne County, also was well-acquainted with the Democratic Mason's chief political rival and Whig critic, William Woodbridge.

When Daniel and his wife Susan Ann Bradley moved to Michigan in 1824, they initially rented farmland from Woodbridge, a Whig who had served as territorial governor and later succeeded Mason in the governor's chair. The property was known as the Livernois Farm.

Daniel did not limit his activities to farming, however.

"Shortly after his arrival in the then-Territory of Michigan, he was commissioned by the U.S. government to open two roads through the dense wilderness which then surrounded

Thompson's Tavern. Daniel Thompson operated this log tavern a half-mile south of "Dearbornville" after serving as Wayne County sheriff. One day, Thompson invited young William Nowlin to the tavern to see his hogs, including a "very cross" sow. In his autobiography about frontier life in Michigan, Nowlin described the occasion: "I suppose Mr. Thompson thought he would have some sport with me, and being generous, he said: 'If the boy will catch one I will give it to him.' I paid no attention to the old sow. but kept my eye on the pig I wanted, and the way I went for it was a caution. I caught it and ran for the fence with the old sow after me. I got over very quickly and was safe with my pig in my arms." *The Bark Covered House, 1876*

Detroit and performed his duties to the entire satisfaction of all parties," according to a local history. "These roads are now the great thorough fares known as the 'Chicago' and 'Gratiot' roads."

Daniel was twice elected sheriff, serving from 1841 to 1845 and carrying out his responsibilities "fearlessly and efficiently." One of his 10 children, Bradley Hemingway Thompson, later held the same position.

William Woodbridge. When Daniel and Susan Bradley arrived in Detroit in 1824, they rented land from governor-to-be William Woodbridge, one of the highest-profile politicians of the day. A self-proclaimed "son of New England," Woodbridge was born during the Revolution and once said, "I inhaled with my first breath an unconquerable aversion to tyranny." He was a member of the Ohio legislature in 1814 when he was appointed secretary of Michigan Territory. During parts of his tenure as secretary, he also served as territorial delegate to Congress and as a territorial Supreme Court judge, provoking criticism that he held too much power. As a Whig, he was later elected Michigan's second governor but resigned to take a seat in the U.S. Senate. He was suggested in 1848 as a potential vice-presidential running mate for Zachary Taylor but, as journalist-author George Weeks put it, "he preferred the life of a recluse and gentleman farmer." Woodbridge's Detroit farm is now the site of Tiger Stadium. *State Archives of Michigan*

After leaving the sheriff's office, Daniel moved to Dearborn, where he ran Thompson's Tavern on the western bank of the Rouge River.

Because of his status as a War of 1812 veteran, he was entitled to 160 acres of bounty land in Dearborn. During that war he had served as a cavalry sergeant stationed at various points on the Niagara Frontier along the Canadian border where, it was later written, he was "an active participant in the excitement of the days."

In his years in Michigan, Daniel also held posts as constable, overseer of highways and member of the state's first gubernatorial canvass. That commitment to public service was part of his life even to the end. He died at age 73 while on Circuit Court jury duty.

"He seemed to be quite a character," great-great-great granddaughter Irene Church observed. "Even in the cemetery he was moved three times."

Erastus Day Sr. and Lucy Willard

To let them grow with the country

The little colony of 32 would-be settlers set out by chartered boat along the Erie Canal to Buffalo, carrying horses, wagons and a full supply of farm implements for the new life they planned in Michigan Territory.

From there it was a stormy three-day passage aboard the steamer *Superior* to Detroit, and three days overland to Armada Township, not far from Romeo.

Erastus Day was among the organizers of that 1827 expedition to Macomb County, seeking opportunities for the children he and his wife Lucy Willard raised. There were only four log houses in Romeo when the anxious, hopeful group arrived.

"The purpose of both Capt. Gad Chamberlin (another leader) and Mr. Day was to give to each of their boys a farm and let them grow up with the country," wrote Dr. J.H. Hollister, whose father John was the group's third organizer. "As land could be had within five miles in any direction from their land-

Erastus Day Jr. and Betsey Day. Erastus Day Jr., was 17 when his family came to the frontier. He helped clear land upon their arrival and earned a yoke of oxen for seven months' labor. He served in the state militia and "fought" in the bloodless Toledo War, the 1835 border dispute between Ohio and Michigan. He later became township supervisor and justice of the peace. In 1836, he married his cousin Betsey, who was a pioneer school teacher in Armada Township. *History of Macomb County, Michigan, 1882 (Erastus Day) and Gerald L. Wolven (Betsey Day)*

ing place at $1.25 an acre, such a purpose was within their means, as it could not have been at the East."

Hollister, who was 3 years old when he traveled to Michigan with the group, wrote his recollections 82 years later.

One of Day's sons, Daniel, also related his memories of those early days on the frontier. He told about their first house made of logs covered with elm bark and a partial floor of bass wood, with holes for windows and doors. "We quietly moved into it without any fireplace or chimney except a hole in the roof for the smoke to escape through," he said.

"Hardly a night passed but we would hear wolves howling in

ERASTUS DAY SR. & LUCY WILLARD

different directions," Daniel continued. He described one incident where a long-legged brown bear was spotted attacking a
family hog: "Bruin made good his escape after having bitten Mr.
Porker so badly that he afterward died."

Erastus Day was among the signers of a December 1829 petition urging President Andrew Jackson to retain Major Thomas
Rowland as federal marshal and a March 1830 petition seeking
to keep James Witherell as territorial secretary.

Lewis Edwards and Patience Garwood

Through an unbroken forest

The bitter winter journey was perilous. There was fear that the wagons would capsize while fording the St. Joseph River. The lead horses injured themselves breaking through the frozen crust along the snow-covered route, leaving a trail of blood "through the unbroken forest."

Lewis Edwards and his wife Patience Garwood survived that arduous January 1827 trek from Ohio to Cass County and prospered.

It seems that the New Jersey-born Lewis was destined to experience frontier life. "He, very early in life, evinced an adventurous tendency and repeatedly expressed to his parents his discontent of home and his eagerness to go West," a county history relates.

When he turned 21, he and a friend set off by foot for Pittsburgh, then traveled by boat to Cincinnati where he worked on

Lewis and Patience Edwards. What could be raised on the land was as important to Lewis Edwards as the land itself. In 1826, he brought a "peacock" plow, set of iron harrow teeth, one-horse plow, scythes, maple sugaring equipment, sickles and a peck of apple seed to the frontier. Over the following years, he bought "improved Durham cattle" from the Ohio Shakers, obtained grafts from fruit trees at his father's New Jersey home and traveled to Ohio for 300 apple trees, 100 pear trees and an unspecified number of raspberry and currant bushes. In 1852, he accompanied his oldest daughter and son-in-law on a six-month journey to Oregon Territory, returning in 1854 to spend the rest of his life on his Cass County farm. *History of Cass County, Michigan, 1882*

a Mississippi River boat. From there he went on to learn carpentry and marry Patience.

But he left his wife with her parents in Ohio to explore the "St. Joseph El Dorado" in Michigan. "Being favorably impressed with the country, he determined to make it his future home." To start, he bought a field of corn that already had been planted, helped other settlers cut wheat and marsh hay, and picked out a farm site on the fertile Pokagon Prairie, "wisely selecting it so as to have an abundance of good timber, especially an excellent maple sugar camp."

Carrying a 30-pound package, he walked back to Ohio to get his wife and infant daughter. Upon their arrival in Michigan, the family stayed with a neighbor while Lewis built a log house. He also planted an orchard with seeds he had carried from Ohio and "had for many years the finest and greatest variety of apples of any man in the county. In pears he was equally successful," according to the county history.

On one occasion he was summoned as Pokagon Township justice of the peace to officiate at a wedding. Although ailing and tired from a just-completed trip, "Squire Edwards," as he was nicknamed, agreed to go. Arriving at the bride's home, he discovered that the couple had no marriage license and refused to perform what he insisted would be an illegal ceremony. Even so, the wedding meal went on as scheduled and Lewis partook of the dinner with other members of the party. The bride and groom then traveled to Cassopolis to get married, and the guests later developed Lewis' illness — mumps.

Crocker Giddings and Orpha Felton

Smitten with the Michigan fever

When Crocker Giddings made an exploratory foray into Michigan in 1827, he was favorably impressed with what he found.

Even so, he returned east and waited another eight years before taking the momentous step of moving his family permanently to the frontier.

In June 1835, Crocker "landed in Detroit with all his earthly possessions, consisting of a few household goods and a family of six children," his oldest son, Alden N. Giddings, recalled more than a half-century later. Crocker had been "smitten with the Michigan fever," as Alden put it in 1897 remarks to the Oakland County Pioneer Society.

Crocker, his Massachusetts-born wife Orpha Felton, and their children made their way westward by steamer across Lake Erie from Buffalo to Detroit. Because Orpha had relatives in the

Alden Navel Giddings, the oldest son of Crocker and Orpha, came to Michigan as a youth. The family arrived in Oakland County with only a "few household goods," he later recalled. Alden is shown here with his wife Sarah Christine Ackert. At various points in his life, he clerked at Friend Walker Tavern, worked as a sheep drover and tried unsuccessfully to farm in Montcalm County —only to discover that his 160 acres were too wet. *James L. Johnson*

Pontiac area, her husband and Alden set out on foot to Oakland County in search of farmland.

"Leaving the rest of the family in Detroit, my father and I made our way to Pontiac on foot, as there was then no railroad," Alden wrote. The family rented farms for several years before buying land of their own in Independence and White Lake townships.

Survival rather than book learning was the priority on the frontier, as Alden explained it. "We were then considered educated if we could read, write, spell and 'figger.' It was not then considered necessary for one to carry a college around in his head in order to be called educated. Utility was looked to, rather than accomplishments."

He also described forms of frontier entertainment, including barn-raisings and house-raisings. "These parties usually ended up either in whiskey or a frolic, or both. At one of these parties,

122

Edward Charles Giddings. The youngest son of Orpha and Crocker Giddings, Edward lived with his parents until their deaths and sold their farm about 15 years later. He then moved to Holly Township in northwest Oakland County and eventually to Benzie County. *James L. Johnson*

two old settlers of Independence, who had imbibed quite freely, entered into a wrestling match. Both fell, one on each side of a log blackened by fire; each immediately grappled into the log swinging it under, thinking it was the other."

Orpha died in 1877 and when Crocker followed three years later, he was eulogized by a Pontiac newspaper as "well known and highly respected" after nearly a half-century in the county.

Dolphin Morris and Susanna Nancy Beaver

Unsolved murders on the frontier

Loneliness. Hardship. Challenge. Murder.

All were part of the rugged life faced by the first pioneers in Van Buren County, Dolphin Morris, his wife Susanna Nancy Beaver and their children.

After traveling to Michigan by lumber wagon in 1828, they spent their first winter with a relative in Cass County. When spring came, they headed for the Little Prairie Ronde area of Decatur Township, southwest of Kalamazoo. Their first home had three small windows and a stick-and-mud chimney.

"For nearly two years he was the only settler in this county. His rude cabin not only sheltered the first white family, but under its roof the first school was taught in the winter of 1833–1834," according to a newspaper account a century later.

In 1832, Dolphin's brother Samuel and several other settlers came to the area but that year proved difficult for the handful of struggling farmers. Their corn crop was destroyed twice by frost,

Dolphin and Susanna Morris. Neither the Virginia-born Dolphin Morris nor his Kentucky-born wife, Susanna Nancy Beaver, were well-schooled — Dolphin's education "was confined to what a youth could learn in about four or six weeks. He learned the alphabet and to write his signature, though not a very legible hand," while Susanna's "was limited to a few months at the district school where she learned to read and write." Even so, the couple had the right stuff to meet the challenges of the wilderness. One 19th century account tells of a difficult trip Dolphin made in 1832 to a mill in Niles: "Encountering a terrible snow-storm as well as very bad roads, he was 14 days making the trip, and when he got home it was with but the fore-wheels of his wagon, his team and a bag of flour." As for Susanna, "many times her courage was put to a severe test" and "many times she was left entirely alone, with her children, to care for all the stock, etc., while her husband was away on business." *History of Berrien & Van Buren Counties, Michigan, 1880*

so Dolphin sent a man, a youth and a horse 100 miles to Fort Defiance, Ohio, to buy two more bushels of seed corn.

The family lays claim to several firsts — some pleasant, others grim.

Susanna — generally called by her middle name Nancy — gave

125

Reverend William Sprague.
Rhode Island-born Rev. William Sprague came to the Morris' isolated home to preach the first sermon in Van Buren County. An itinerant Methodist minister, Sprague served in a series of church posts in Oakland, St. Joseph, Monroe, Farmington, Plymouth, Tecumseh and eventually Kalamazoo. He later won a seat in Congress. His 1848 election as an anti-slavery Free Soil-Whig candidate signaled a significant change in Michigan politics which would lead to the

founding of the Republican party in Jackson and, as an historian put it, to "the overthrow of the old order of things in the state." *State Archives of Michigan*

birth to the first white child born in the county. The infant named Lewis lived only a few months however, and thus became the county's first recorded death.

The family also provided Van Buren County's first hotel, first church service and first school. Weary travelers along the trail between Niles and Grand Rapids often stopped by their log house for food and shelter. And they invited an itinerant Methodist minister, Rev. William Sprague, to preach the county's first sermon in their home. Sprague later represented Michigan in Congress.

In addition, the family was intimately and tragically involved with the county's first known murder — the celebrated and officially unsolved 1879 slaying of their son and daughter-in-law, Charles and Esther.

The victims were considered wealthy by the standards of the

126

Charles and Esther Jones Morris. Charles Morris, the youngest son of Dolphin and Susanna, was murdered with his wife Esther in 1879. A county history melodramatically details the crime, which occurred shortly after the couple went to bed for the night. Charles was "called to the door, and there shot twice through the heart by a cowardly assassin. The fiend, not satisfied with the blood of one victim, entered the house, and immediately opened fire upon Mrs. Morris, whom he met coming, with a small revolver in hand, to her husband's rescue. She retreated to her bedroom, pursued by the fiend, who shot her twice through the body; she then entered a closet adjoining, where she fell and was shot twice more. Thus ended one of the most horrible tragedies ever perpetrated in any civilized community." *History of Berrien & Van Buren Counties, Michigan, 1880*

day. One later account of the fatal shooting reported that "nothing of value was carried away, although valuable property was within reach. Theories as to motive spring up like weeds but the true facts have never been commonly known."

Mary M. Stump, a great-great granddaughter of Susanna and Dolphin, says the killer's identity is no secret to the family. The murderer, her grandmother confided many years ago, was a man who had been rebuffed when he sought to buy some of

127

Morris homestead. This is the comfortable frame home built by Dolphin and Susanna Morris on their Decatur Township farmstead. The farm grew due to "prudence and economy" to 1,100 acres, and the couple gave each of their children a nearby farm. After their deaths, the house passed to their youngest son Charles, and there he and his wife were murdered. The picture also shows the horse "which carried the assassin from this frightful scene." The house known as the Morris murder mansion was destroyed in a 1962 fire. *History of Berrien & Van Buren Counties, Michigan, 1880*

Charles' prime farmland. After the double slaying, the killer stole one of the victims' prize horses, rode it hard 40 miles to South Bend, Ind., then fled west — never to return to Michigan. The horse was found "in a very jaded condition" the morning after the murders.

Esther Morris' dresser. Morris descendant Mary Stump points to a bullet hole in the dresser of Esther Morris, who was murdered with her husband Charles in their home in 1879. *Dick Derrick, The Detroit News*

Private Pinkerton detectives were hired and a $2,000 reward was offered but the killer was not captured. Esther's marble-topped walnut dresser with a bullet hole from the shooting is still owned by the family.

Chester Wall and Christiana Frink

In search of a Capitol site

Sandstone and Barry don't even rate a dot on the official Michigan highway map, but Chester Wall dreamed of making what was once a small but bustling Jackson County community into the state's capital.

Chester, an immigrant from New York, arrived in 1829 to buy farmland. As the first settler in Sandstone Township, he cut rails to mark the boundaries of his new property and built a log cabin. Then it was back to the East for his wife Christiana Frink and their two young daughters.

Returning home, their wagon mired in a creek within sight of the cabin, so Chester placed the girls on nearby rocks while he extricated the wagon.

As Chester worked the farm, other settlers including a tavern keeper, a blacksmith and a physician followed. A log school was erected, as were a church and two water-powered sawmills. The

Chester Wall was an early and enthusiastic booster of his adopted Michigan community, Sandstone Township in Jackson County. His efforts to persuade the Legislature to designate it as the state capital failed. *Frances A. Gork & Irving Wheeler*

community known as Sandstone Corners was renamed Barry and grew larger than nearby Jackson.

Chester and Christiana contributed to the growth by having three more children. In addition, Chester's parents John and Sally Wall joined them in 1834. And seven of his nine brothers and sisters moved to Michigan, settling in Jackson, Eaton and Washtenaw counties.

Chester was elected township supervisor and served on the county's first grand jury.

A year after Christiana's 1840 death, he married local school teacher Rachel Rillou. He and Rachel had seven daughters, five of whom went on to college in an era when it was unusual for girls to even complete high school.

Barry continued to grow for a while. It served as a station for stagecoaches traveling between Chicago and Detroit and, at one point, boasted five taverns, a bank and a wagonmaker's shop.

Chester helped prepare the plat for a village that —local residents hoped —would be selected as Michigan's seat of government. "If the plat had gone through, some of the streets

131

The Wall home was built in 1859, 30 years after Chester arrived from New York as a frontier farmer. It replaced the original log cabin on his Jackson County property. The picture taken about a decade after his death shows one of his daughters, two grandchildren and a son-in-law. *Frances A. Gork & Irving Wheeler*

would have been named for him and the family," said descendant Frances A. Gork. A site for the hoped-for capitol building was even chosen and dubbed "Capitol Hill."

Of course, the Legislature chose Lansing as the capital city instead. Still, Chester Wall remained loyal to Barry until his death in 1884.

Pierre A. Guillot and Mary Esther Fournier

Mystery upon mystery

Pierre A. Guillot was a mystery man.

Questions linger about when he came to Michigan from Canada, his whereabouts in 1850 —even the date and place of his death and burial.

A blacksmith by trade, Pierre was the son of a War of 1812 veteran who, as a citizen of British-ruled Canada, fought against the recently independent United States.

But he left Ontario and crossed the Detroit River for a new life in the neighboring new nation. In 1830, he married Mary Esther Fournier in Detroit's St. Anne's Church.

In 1836, he moved to Saginaw at a time when travel between the two cities was difficult. "The area north of Detroit was all swamp, and it was necessary to take a boat to Mt. Clemens or further north in order to travel overland. A horse and rider could get through, but any household possessions had to be

First Corps of Engineers and Mechanics Monument. Pierre Guillot, a Canadian immigrant to Detroit and Saginaw, served during the Civil War in the 1st Corps of Engineers and Mechanics, one of 44 regiments raised by the state. The corps, which was organized in Marshall and disbanded in Jackson, "was intended to be principally employed in the numerous kinds of mechanical and engineering work incident to the operation of an army. . . . It was also armed with infantry weapons and, whenever called on, its members showed themselves as prompt in battle as they were

skillful in labor," according to a 19th century history. It built railroads and steamboat landings, fought in the Battle of Chickamauga and marched with Gen. William Tecumseh Sherman across Georgia to the sea. This memorial monument was erected in 1912 on the northeast corner of the Capitol grounds in Lansing. *Michigan Capitol Committee*

moved by water," according to great-great-granddaughter Marcia Van Auken Mason.

Pierre is believed to have followed a brother-in-law, Harvey Williams, north, Mason said. "I think that attracted Pierre. They had a mill and needed blacksmiths."

It was Williams who built Saginaw's first steam sawmill, using the engine that had powered *Walk-in-the-Water*, the first steamboat on the upper Great Lakes. Historian Bruce Catton gives this account of Williams' enterprise: "With considerable mechanical ingenuity, he devised a rig by which the old side-wheeler engine could operate a gate saw, and the lumber indus-

PIERRE A. GUILLOT & MARY ESTHER FOURNIER

try took a step in the right direction; but the step was short, because this mill was slow and clumsy and could do little more than meet the needs of settlers in the immediate vicinity."

Once settled in Saginaw, he apparently became a naturalized citizen and changed his first name to Peter.

Even in the United States, Pierre remembered his roots on the opposite side of the border. He successfully applied in 1842 to Canada's governor-general for a 100-acre land grant his father was entitled to for service with the British in the War of 1812.

According to a Saginaw County history, he was a Whig candidate for coroner in 1844.

One unsolved mystery is Pierre's whereabouts in 1850, when his family was counted without him in local census records. His descendants speculate that he may have returned to Detroit or Canada to work and, thus, was away when the census was taken. He reappeared in the 1860 census. The county history shows that he served during the Civil War in the 1st Corps of Engineers and Mechanics and in the 8th Cavalry.

Then there's the mystery of his death.

Two unidentified Guillot family members were buried in a Saginaw cemetery between 1860 — when Pierre was last included in a census — and 1873, when his wife Mary was described as a widow living with her son-in-law. Pierre may have been one of those interred there, possibly having died elsewhere and having his body brought back home.

Luther Pond and Sarah White

Always westward

As America moved westward, so did Luther Pond.

Born in Connecticut in 1790, he was living in New York State by the time the War of 1812 erupted. In his early 20s, Luther enlisted in the militia and marched with Capt. Elias Hull's regiment in 1812 and 1813.

Military service already was a tradition with the family because Luther's grandfather had fought in the Revolutionary War.

Already well into middle age, Luther uprooted his family and headed further west to settle in Kalamazoo County's Comstock Township sometime in the early 1830s.

When Luther arrived in Michigan with Sarah White, his Connecticut-born wife, he was probably a farmer. By the end of the decade, he was located a bit farther west, in Cass County's Wayne Township, near Dowagiac.

According to a handwritten entry in the family Bible, he died

George Miller Pond, (*previous page*) son of southwestern Michigan settlers Luther and Sarah Pond, served in the Civil War and became a store owner and restaurant keeper. He is shown here with his wife Mary Ann Murphy, four of their children and a granddaughter. *Mary Roma Nowak*

there at age 53 from a "severe blow to the breast." His death took a week, and the family believes the fatal injury occurred while he was cutting trees. The widowed Sarah later received 160 acres of bounty land from the federal government based on Luther's War of 1812 service.

Their son George Miller Pond also performed military duty by fighting in Company D of the 11th Regiment of the Michigan Infantry during the Civil War.

George later owned a general store with a small restaurant, probably having only a table or two. Appropriately for a Pond, his store was located in Van Buren County, one of the westernmost counties in the Lower Peninsula.

And at age 75, a disability pension application showed him living much further west in Colorado. He eventually returned to Michigan and died at the state Soldier and Sailors' Home in Grand Rapids.

Samuel Babcock and Elizabeth Groves

Undeterred by the plague

Samuel Babcock's first glimpse of Michigan had come when he "carried a musket" during the War of 1812, and he decided to return. The frontier was a land of opportunity for some, but frontier life could be cruel.

That's what Samuel discovered when an 1832 cholera epidemic wiped out more than 200 Oakland County residents, including his wife and four children.

Bereaved, Samuel returned to his native New York. There at age 45 — an age at which many people of the time died rather than wed — he married Elizabeth Groves and fathered another child, Elisha John Jay Babcock.

Michigan still held a grip on Samuel's heart, despite tragic memories of the cholera epidemic. So in 1836, Samuel and his new family left New York for Jackson, where they farmed until moving to St. Joseph County. They ended up in Nottawa Township in 1854, among the first settlers there.

Elizabeth Babcock's dishes.
When Elizabeth Babcock emigrated west to Michigan, she defied her husband's order to leave her treasured dishes behind. Instead, she hid them in barrels of flour for secrecy and protection on the difficult journey west. Her great-great-great-granddaughter Dorothy Shane shows off some of Elizabeth's dishes, now family heirlooms. *Susan Tusa, The Detroit News*

At the time of his death at age 85, Samuel would be remembered as a hard-working farmer who donated land for the local school and cemetery. One account told how he "lived and labored (in St. Joseph County) for a period of 20 years and then closed his eyes upon earthly scenes."

His widow Elizabeth collected a pension based on his military service until her death at age 100.

Elizabeth was resourceful in her own right. For example, although Samuel refused to allow his wife to take her treasured dishes from New York, she hid them in barrels of flour. They survived the arduous trip to Michigan and remain family heirlooms.

Jean Baptist Charboneau and Mary Martin

Farmer and fiddler

Bell is now a ghost town, abandoned by its people, its buildings crumbled and swallowed up by the woods of the Thumb. The same area was wilderness when Jean Baptist Charboneau arrived as the first settler in what would become the logging community of Bell.

Jean was a native of Quebec who emigrated by way of New York State to Sault Ste. Marie in 1830 and then moved to St. Ignace, where he married Mary Martin.

The couple made their way to Presque Isle Township on the shores of Lake Huron and became the first landowners in the village-to-be of Bell.

"The land was sandy and stony, making it difficult to grow on, so Jean raised cattle. In the winter his animals were fed on wild hay that Jean would cut in the fall," according to a history of Bell. He also carried the mail by dog team from Saginaw to Mackinaw City in the winters of 1857 to 1863. Mary was

The Bell Cemetery, where Jean and Mary Charboneau are buried, was started when a local man was slain by his lover's irate husband. Located in Mackinaw State Forest, it was restored and rededicated in 1989, more than a half-century after the village was abandoned to the woods. *Lew Sowa, Alpena News*

described as "an immaculate housekeeper. The pine floor of their house was scrubbed with lye until it became clean and white."

Bell grew, at least for a while, until it reached about 100 inhabitants. The surrounding forests of white pine, Norway pine and hemlock made it possible for a local lumbering industry to develop, supplying fuel to lake steamers, logs for two sawmills and wood to make barrel hoops. The village also boasted a brickmaking business and served as a port for commercial fishing boats. Efforts to drill for oil there proved unsuccessful.

The site of the abandoned village, including virgin stands of

Commemorative stone. The names of "John" and Mary Charboneau are inscribed on a memorial stone at the restored Bell Cemetery. *Robert E. Haltiner, Jesse Besser Museum*

red and white pine, is now within the Besser Bell Natural Area in the Mackinaw State Forest, a gift from an Alpena industrialist who had acquired the property in 1965. Its cemetery is the final resting place for Jean and Mary.

When Jean died in 1909, one newspaper put his age at 103. The family believes he was closer to 93, but nobody knows his age for sure. It is known, however, that he enjoyed playing the fiddle at Saturday night square dances until his death.

And it was only two years later than a sure sign of Bell's own impending death appeared —the closing of the village post office.

Jacob Freidrich Heck and Katarina Ott

It took many years but they worked hard.

The unknown of the distant Michigan frontier offered opportunity, something that Jacob Freidrich Heck and his wife Katarina Ott couldn't find along the familiar Rhine River in their native Germany.

While working in a vineyard there, they learned from friends and relatives that a whole farm could be purchased in America for the price of a few acres of German soil. Aware they could never afford to own property in their homeland, Katarina and Freidrich — as her husband was known — braved a three-month voyage across the Atlantic.

Upon their arrival in 1830, they set out for the shores of Lake Erie in Monroe County, where five other German families already had settled. There in Monroe Township, Freidrich began the task of clearing the woods to develop a farm. "It took many years to clear the trees and stumps, but they worked hard," according to a family history.

144

Katarina Heck. Katarina and Jacob Heck had 12 children, including two sets of twins. Together the couple cleared the wooded land to establish a farm still owned by the Heck family. *Nancy Heck Huggins*

145

Katherine, Gottfried & Julianna Heck. Gottfried Heck and his twin sister Katherine, shown knitting in this late 19th century picture, sailed across the Atlantic at age 2 in their mother Katarina's arms. At the spinning wheel is Gottfried's wife Julianna Knab, daughter of the first German settler in Monroe County, Simeon Knab. *Nancy Heck Huggins*

But there was more to life than work. The growing number of German-speaking immigrants in the area felt a spiritual void, so 10 families invited Rev. Frederick Schmidt of Ann Arbor to preach to them.

The itinerant Lutheran pastor traveled by horseback to Monroe for services once every eight weeks, starting on the fourth Sunday of Advent in 1833. After his first service, he wrote, "On Sunday morning I gave a sermon to these dear people, who shed

Reverend Frederick Schmidt. Described as "infected with a missionary's wanderlust, Rev. Frederick Schmidt —or Freidrich Schmid —was an Ann Arbor-based Lutheran pastor who traveled around the Michigan frontier to minister to the spiritual needs of German immigrants, including Katarina Ott and Jacob Freidrich Heck. As a 27-year-old pastor in 1833, he began German congregations near Ann Arbor and Scio. He wrote to Germany about his first trip to Monroe: "I went there in the company of a guide who showed me the way. We had hardly gone two miles when the road became so bad that we believed we would become stuck, and we had some 40 miles to go. Since there isn't a single inn on this highway for a distance of 10 miles, only here and there a log cabin, we had difficulty finding lodging. Finally as it was already night we found a house and barn where we lodged." He later helped select the site of Michigan's best-known German community, Frankenmuth. *State Archives of Michigan*

many tears at my proclaiming the holy word in the forest." On other Sundays, Freidrich or another member of the congregation would read sermons from a prayer book bought from Schmidt.

In 1838, the immigrants incorporated as Evangelical Lutheran Zoar Church and soon built a log church to worship in.

Freidrich died in his adopted country in 1861, more than three decades after daring to challenge an unknown land and an alien culture to make a new life for his family. Katarina's death came in 1877.

Nicholas Groves and Clarinda Holbrook

From sailor to settler

The treacherous whaling routes of the Pacific Ocean are leagues from the fertile soil of the Michigan frontier, but Nicholas Groves spent four years on a whaling expedition before he decided to become a farmer.

The native Vermonter went to sea at age 20 in search of whale oil. The four-year hunt proved "a profitable one in the accumulation of oil," according to a family history, but problems arose on the homebound journey when the ship was condemned in Jamaica as unseaworthy. In a midnight escapade, Nicholas and another sailor smuggled two barrels of oil onto a Spanish vessel and sailed to Nantucket, Mass., where he worked as a tailor.

Determined to stay firmly on land, he bought half his father's Massachusetts farm and married Roxa Stearns. She died in childbirth in 1824.

Seven years later, Nicholas headed west with his second wife,

Black Hawk. Sauk chief Black Hawk, a Potawatomi by birth, was a renowned warrior who fought on the side of the British during the War of 1812. When Black Hawk resisted government efforts to relocate his tribe from Illinois to a western reservation, war broke out on the frontier in 1832. Nicholas Groves alerted his Washtenaw County neighbors to the hostilities. The fighting did not reach what is now Michigan, but parts of Michigan Territory in what is now southeastern Wisconsin were directly affected. A Michigan militia regiment, the Detroit City Guards and mounted volunteers started marching toward Chicago; they only reached Saline before they were called back to Detroit and disbanded. The Sauk were defeated and Black Hawk was taken captive, eventually dying on a reservation in Iowa. *Michigan as a Province, Territory & State, 1906*

Clarinda Holbrook, and five children. The family arrived in Northfield Township, Washtenaw County, where they purchased 160 acres of land.

In 1832, it was Nicholas who alerted the militia when the alarm spread about the Black Hawk War, a conflict that had erupted when a Sauk tribe led by Chief Black Hawk resisted Army efforts to relocate them to a reservation.

The following year, local citizens elected Nicholas overseer of the poor at the first township meeting.

His son William Parley Groves was drafted into the militia in 1835 when Ohio and Michigan Territory seesawed on the brink of war over ownership of the Toledo Strip. William later worked as a local postmaster, served on the school board, helped found the Washtenaw Pomological Society devoted to growing apples and contributed heavily to the Union cause during the Civil War.

Leonard Keene Jr. and Alice Shaffer

Always looking for something better

Unlike most early Michigan settlers, Leonard Keene Jr. headed north rather than west to reach the territory.

The North Carolina native moved to Ohio early in childhood to live with an older brother after the sudden deaths of their parents. According to family accounts, his father was killed in a fire and his mother died soon afterward.

In Ohio, Leonard met Alice —also known as Alcey —Shaffer, and the couple married in 1831.

In that same year, the newlyweds "started for the great west and the Garden of Eden to be found in southwestern Michigan," a local newspaper reported when Leonard died almost five decades later.

The couple sought their Garden of Eden in Calvin Township, Cass County, where they started to farm and raise a family. Leonard became active in the Methodist Church there.

"They, like most people back them, were very sociable with

Lewis Cass. When Leonard and Alice Keene settled in Michigan, they chose a county named for one of the most prominent American political leaders of the early 19th century, Lewis Cass. Journalist-author George Weeks wrote: "Nearly 200 years after he had come to the state, Lewis Cass still loomed as one of the foremost names in state history and politics, as well as Michigan's most eminent statesman." As an explorer, Cass traveled from Detroit by birch bark canoe to Minnesota in 1820 and later promoted Michigan as worthy of settlement. As a soldier, Cass served as a general in the War of 1812 and testified at the court-martial of territorial Gov. William Hull, who had surrendered Detroit to the British without firing a shot in defense of the city. As a politician, he was Michigan's second territorial governor, twice a U.S. senator after statehood and the unsuccessful 1848 Democratic nominee for president. As a government leader, he served as Andrew Jackson's Secretary of War, minister to France under Jackson and Martin Van Buren, and Secretary of State under James Buchanan. *State Archives of Michigan*

their families," said Avis Keene, whose husband Richard is their great-great-grandson. Looking back more than a century and a half, she said no documents have been found to specify what attracted the Keenes to Michigan, but she believes it was the same motivation that drew so many others: "It was always to find better land to find better living. They were always looking for something better."

Peter S. Keene, the son of Leonard and Alice, represented the family's second generation in Michigan. Born in 1835, two years before statehood, he later moved further north to Allegan County and served in the Union Army during the Civil War.

Peter Crebassa and Nancy Rosseau

I did to the best of my ability

It took three years of persistent requests before Peter Crebassa lured noted missionary Father —later Bishop —Frederic Baraga to L'Anse on the shore of chill Lake Superior.

Peter had brought a French Bible to L'Anse, at the southern end of Keweenaw Bay when he set up a trading post for the American Fur Co. "An old chief named Penanshi (or Benanshi) came to see me every Sunday," he would write later. "The old chief used to request me to read to him from the book and explain it, which I did to the best of my ability. He desired to know if I could get a priest to come here."

So Peter began a campaign in 1840 to persuade Baraga, the only priest in that part of the country, to visit from the mission in La Pointe, Wisc., 180 miles to the west.

In 1843, Baraga agreed to come. In a letter addressed to "my dear friend" Peter Crebassa, the missionary said, "There's now three years' resistance to the invitation to go to L'Anse, for I

Peter & Nancy Crebassa. Peter and his wife Nancy Rousseau Crebassa came to L'Anse to establish a trading post. Before settling there, Peter's duties as an agent for the American Fur Co. had taken him along Lake Superior from Sault Ste. Marie to Fond du Lac, Wisc. As a late 19th century Upper Peninsula history recalled, "At that early day, an occasional trading post was all there was to suggest the approach of civilization. The wild scenes he must have passed through, the perilous voyages that he was obliged to make in the frail craft of that period, were all fraught with danger and adventure." *State Archives of Michigan and Upper Peninsula Catholic Historical Society, Marquette*

don't like to leave my children, and now I cannot resist any more, for I think it is the will of God that I must go."

As Peter described the long-awaited visit, "I had arranged everything and had a number of Indians camping in wigwams

L'Anse trading post site. The marker on this monument reads: "This monument marks the site of the first trading post established for the American Fur Trading Company by Peter Crebassa in 1837." The plaque was presented in 1938 by the students of L'Anse Township Schools National Youth Administration. *Baraga County Historical Society and G. Glover Juntunen*

Bishop Frederic Baraga. Known as the "Indian Apostle of the Northwest," Slovenia-born Father Frederic Baraga established the Roman Catholic mission in L'Anse at the behest of Peter Crebassa, as well as other missions in Michigan's Upper and Lower Peninsulas and in Wisconsin. He wrote a landmark grammar and dictionary of the Chippewa language in a small room adjoining the L'Anse church. Later he was appointed the first bishop for northern Michigan. The county was eventually named in his honor. *Bishop Baraga Association, Marquette*

on my place. I gave Father Baraga half my house to use as a chapel, and for the purpose of teaching the Indians." When it was time for the priest to return to Wisconsin 20 days later, Peter furnished a canoe and two men to accompany him. Back in Wisconsin, Baraga sent a thank-you letter to Peter with a set of beads for his wife Nancy Rosseau.

Baraga came back to L'Anse that fall to establish a permanent mission, with a log church, school and a few small houses for his new converts. It was Baraga's fifth and final Indian mission.

Peter, who had been born in Quebec and educated in France, was to remain in L'Anse for the rest of his life, along with Nancy, whom he had married in 1837 in Sault Ste. Marie.

In L'Anse, Peter organized the settlement and established a trading post built of pine logs with a cedar shake roof. Enough supplies were brought in each summer from Mackinaw City to last through the harsh Upper Peninsula winters. According to

Baraga statue. This hand-wrought brass statue of Bishop Frederic Baraga overlooks Keweenaw Bay at the Shrine of the Snowshoe Priest, located between the communities of L'Anse and Baraga. It was designed by sculptor Jack Anderson. *Michigan Travel Commission*

The Pinery, an Ojibway burial ground near L'Anse, dates from the 19th century when Indians in this area were the subject of conversion efforts by both the Catholics and the Methodists. Evangelical activities along Keweenaw Bay began at least as early as 1832, when John Sunday, a Methodist Chippewa, arrived. Two years later, fellow Methodist John Clark built a school and mission house that would develop into the Zeba Indian United Methodist Church. *Michigan Travel Commission*

his journal, he bought furs of 1,122 martens, eight bears, nine foxes, 75 beaver, 74 mink, 32 otter, 15 fisher and 160 muskrats in November 1840. However, the fur trade would decline in the following years due to increased settlement and the opening of copper and iron mines in the region.

He served as postmaster until 1882, using part of the trading post as the post office. He also became an officer of the school district and helped operate the Michigamme iron mine.

Philo Galpin and Jane Townsend

With patience and fortitude

History tells us that Philo Galpin and his wife Jane Townsend "endured the privation incident to pioneer life with patience and fortitude when they first arrived at their new home."

There were few other settlers in 1832 when the Galpins arrived in Washtenaw County's Superior Township east of Ann Arbor. Although no nearby schoolhouse yet existed, classes were being taught for the few local children.

Philo had been born in Canada in 1804 but moved with his family at age 9 to New York. There he met his future wife, and they farmed in that state until the westward bug bit.

Their descendants believe Philo made an exploratory trip to Michigan Territory early in 1832. Pleased with what he saw, he returned east to sell his farm and bring his family west.

Philo's parents, Nathan and Flora Galpin, emigrated from New York as well but chose to settle in Macomb County with other relatives. Philo apparently chose Superior Township because Jane's relatives had moved there not long before.

Philo fell ill about a year after they arrived to farm what was then "240 acres of oak openings." What was forest land would eventually become a productive farm. In 1837, Philo and Jane began building their substantial farmhouse of handmade bricks — hauled by horse cart from Detroit — and hand-hewn timbers.

According to family tradition, Jane enjoyed smoking clay pipes, several of which were dug up in the yard of that home over the years.

Philo was elected justice of the peace, an accomplishment that a county history attributes to the "industry, integrity and good will" that enabled him to win "the confidence of his fellow citizens."

William C. Reed and Sarah Beebe

Energetic and industrious

Born near the site of the Battle of Bunker Hill, William C. Reed had adventure in his blood.

At the age of 20, he "shipped aboard a whaler and led the life of a sailor," according to an historical account. After his return to shore, William visited his grandparents in New York, where he met David Beebe, who was then preparing to move to Michigan Territory. William joined the expedition to Oakland County.

There, in 1832, he married Beebe's schoolteacher daughter, Sarah — also known as Sally Ann — in Farmington Hills. Then in 1836 the couple headed north to farm 160 acres in Berlin Township, Ionia County, making a rugged journey that required cutting a road through the wilds.

"On the Sunday following his arrival, with the assistance of four men, he erected a log house on his place," one account said. That task proved far from easy because all the lumber had to be

Alonzo Sessions. When William Reed arrived in remote Ionia County in 1836, he was befriended by Alonzo Sessions, who had built the second log cabin in Berlin Township a year earlier. Once Reed's cabin was finished, the two men "set out with ox teams for a trip eastward in search of provisions and for a good share of the way to Lyons had to cut out the road," according to one account. A former school teacher and store clerk, Sessions later became township supervisor, Ionia County sheriff, bank president, state representative and eventu-

ally the Republican lieutenant governor. His 800-acre farm was described as "well cared for and valuable." *State Archives of Michigan*

transported by canoe from the sawmill "a few boards at a time" across a river.

Obtaining supplies for the homestead also proved difficult, and it took William 12 days to obtain provisions from White Lake Township in Oakland County, a trip that now takes only two hours by car.

William prospered as a farmer. A "substantial building" replaced the original log house. "He was energetic and industrious, and from having funds barely sufficient to make his first purchase from the government, he accumulated a handsome property." In addition to farming, he owned a mill, the site of which he acquired in exchange for six sheep. He also served as highway commissioner.

After his wife's death, he remarried twice. There are conflicting records as to whether he fathered 10 or 11 children.

Although William had survived the rigors of the Michigan frontier, he died violently at the hands of a tenant who owed him money. The tenant struck him on the hip with an ax head, grabbed him by the throat, threw him to the ground and stomped on his chest. Seriously wounded, he died a few days later at age 67.

John Reno and Marie Laubacher

Not a farmer by inclination

Retail advertising and customer relations are not recent inventions, as John Reno's display ad in the 1837 Detroit City Directory demonstrated.

The heading described Reno as a "Dealer in Groceries, Provisions, Wines and Spirits" at the corner of Atwater and St. Antoine. The ad went on to say that Reno "respectfully returns thanks to the citizens of Detroit for the liberal share of public patronage he has received since his commencement in the above business, and he assures them that he still continues to keep every article in his line of the very best quality, and at the lowest cash prices."

Born as Jean Renaud in 1808, he was educated in his native France, then made a six-week sailing voyage to the United States in 1828. Initially he settled in upstate New York, and although a tailor by trade, worked there on a farm until 1832.

"In that year he came to Detroit, journeying by boat by way

John Reno. French-born John Reno became a successful Detroit merchant who proudly advertised his wares as of "the very best quality, and at the lowest cash prices." Active in politics, he served as city assessor, tax collector and member of the Michigan House of Representatives. *Nan Reno*

of the Erie Canal and the Great Lakes, as no railroad transportation was then available," according to a history of Detroit and Wayne County. The city had only about 3,000 inhabitants when he arrived.

It was in Detroit that he married his first wife Marie Laubacher, who had been born in France of German ancestry. After her death during childbirth in 1851, he wed Mary Angley Mayer, a native of Switzerland. He had nine children during the two marriages.

John's first property purchase was a 40-acre parcel of government land on Gratiot Avenue, "which land was then a wilderness. He was not a farmer by inclination, so it was not long before he opened a small grocery store at the foot of St. Antoine Street and also conducted a small boarding house," the local history relates.

A deeply religious man, John donated land for church use. He also was active in civic and political affairs. For example, he became city assessor, tax collector and school board member, helped organize a volunteer company of the Detroit Fire Department and served a term as a Democratic member of the state House of Representatives.

Both Reno Avenue in Detroit and Renaud Road in Grosse Pointe Woods were named for him.

Peter Fagan and Eliza Laura Dains

Careful and industrious

The marriage of Peter Fagan, an Irish immigrant who helped build the Erie Canal, to Eliza Laura Dains, a New York-born descendant of early Pennsylvania Quakers, symbolized the blend of cultures and heritages on the Michigan frontier. They were among the first settlers in Holly Township.

After their wedding before Justice of the Peace Ira Alger – the first such ceremony in the community – the newlyweds loaded up their ox-drawn wagon and headed to the farm where Peter was living in a small shanty.

"Mr. Fagan had for some time 'kept bachelor's hall' in this imposing edifice, and his newly made bride, perhaps remembering the old saying 'what is sauce for the goose is sauce for the gander,' correctly reasoned that she could live in it for a time if he could," an Oakland County history relates.

The shanty had a large fireplace, bed, flour barrel and pork barrel, and "it was a cause for thankfulness in those days to be the possessors of a barrel of pork or a barrel of flour, although either could be purchased for $3." Six months after their wedding, Peter and Eliza moved into a more spacious log house he built on the farm.

Peter's move to the frontier actually had its roots back in 1823 when he arrived in the United States from Ireland with his parents and his brothers. After a decade in New York, the family moved to northwest Oakland County and bought heavily timbered land at $1.25 an acre from the federal government.

Upon arrival in the United States, Peter became a blaster on the Erie Canal and worked on railroad construction. After settling in Michigan, he helped build the Detroit & Saginaw Turnpike, a military road.

Peter developed a reputation as a "careful and industrious farmer." Success was attributed to "patient toil, together with a rigid practice of economy, and a faculty for making everything go its utmost extent." He is recorded as "a man of such excellent business qualifications and sound judgment."

One story is told how he cast the deciding vote in an election for township supervisor. When the disgruntled loser asked who was responsible, Peter blamed another voter. The loser promptly knocked down the scapegoat. "As the latter was an excessive stammerer, he did not have a chance to explain before (the loser's) fist laid him low. It is not related whether amicable relations were afterwards resumed, nor that (the scapegoat) ever learned who had made him the bruised victim of a practical joke."

Over the years, Peter served as township supervisor, clerk, assessor, drain commissioner and highway commissioner. He was instrumental in getting a local post office opened and selected its name, Holly Mills.

Hiram Seger and Leah Elizabeth Burdge

A lot of nerve

It's said that Hiram Seger and his wife Leah Elizabeth Burdge must have had courage to make the westward trek to Michigan Territory with seven children.

"They thought maybe this land was better, that there was more opportunity to get ahead," descendant Frank H. Seger said. "They loaded everything up in two wagons. They took the Erie Canal and then crossed Lake Erie by boat. They must have had a lot of courage. That's a lot of nerve."

Their journey began in 1833 in New York, where Connecticut-born Hiram and New Jersey-born Leah owned a farm. A family history notes, "There had been a large migration from New York to Michigan at that time but the record does not indicate if friends and acquaintances were there to welcome the newcomers."

In 1834, a presidential land grant gave the family 160 acres in Redford, Wayne County, based on Hiram's status as a military

Seger family. Hiram and Elizabeth Seger settled in Wayne County, while their son William later chose Livingston County after his release from a Confederate prisoner-of-war camp at the end of the Civil War. Their descendant Frank H. Seger displays a picture of his ancestors. *Dale Young, The Detroit News*

veteran. The couple had six more children after settling in Michigan.

Hiram was in the middle of three Seger generations with major war experience. His father Joseph had joined the Continental Army in 1776 and fought in the Revolutionary War until his discharge in 1779.

At age 17, Hiram was drafted in the War of 1812 and

wounded in battle. When he was discharged for a disability after being thrown from a horse, he was given a hand-carved wooden cane by the commander.

One son, Michigan-born William Henry Harrison Seger, spent four years with the Union Army during the Civil War. Initially, he signed up in Marquette for 90 days but reenlisted for the duration of the war, fighting in such battles as Gettsyburg, Antietam and Chancellorsville. He was captured by the enemy and spent 10 months in the Confederacy's infamous Andersonville, Ga., prison camp.

Returning to Michigan after his release, William farmed for a while in Redford, then resettled in Brighton where he served as village president and ran a well-digging business.

Pliny Atherton Skinner and Delia Alvord

Suffering the hardships and privations usual to the lot of the first settlers

Although still frontier in 1835, Oakland County may have been a bit too crowded for Pliny Atherton Skinner's taste. So he moved further into the wilderness in search of more remote land to farm.

Ten years earlier, the orphaned Skinner had come as a teenager to Michigan from northern New York with his sister, uncle, aunt and two cousins. The uncle, Shubael Atherton, gave what is now Waterford its name "on account of the numerous beautiful lakes within its borders," according to a local historical account.

But at 27, Pliny felt the urge to move on and set his sights on a more isolated area in Shiawassee County, where he began clearing a tract of land. Unexpectedly Shubael, who had raised him since his mother's death, came by.

Skinner "dropped his axe" to accompany Shubael and another uncle on an exploratory hike along an Indian trail to

Pliny and Delia Skinner. Both Pliny and Delia Skinner were born in New York. Pliny became one of the first property owners in Burton Township. He and his uncles Shubael and Perus Atherton "began their labors by cutting out a road sufficient for the passage of a team and wagon. The three families passed the winter alone in the wilderness, and formed the nucleus of what was destined to be a thriving settlement of 30 families ere the lapse of the ensuing 12 months," according to local history. This picture shows their original cabin, their successful farm and their residence in Flint. *History of Genesee County, Michigan, 1879*

the Flint River area of Genesee County. After a few days' investigation, the trio decided to buy land along the Thread River in what is now the Flint suburb of Burton.

"Here he and his wife began their pioneer life in the woods, suffering the hardships and privations usual to the lot of the first settlers in a timbered country, and laid the foundations for a

175

pleasant home and a comfortable competence," as an 1879 book about Genesee County's prominent residents put it.

Pliny and his wife Delia Alvord were among the first settlers of Burton and needed help from friends in Flint to build their log house. The Skinners awoke some mornings in that first log cabin along the river to find Indians sleeping inside for warmth. He labored to clear about 100 acres, "mostly with his own hands," built neat fences and outbuildings, and their farm prospered.

Three uncles —Shubael, Adonijah and Perus Atherton — lived on adjacent farms, and the area became known as the Atherton Settlement. A county history tells of community difficulties during the early years:

> The removal from New York to Michigan and the purchase of their lands had, in most instances, exhausted their all. Soon their resources were gone, eaten up; poor crops followed an unfavorable season, and all were poor in common. Destitution and privations existed upon all sides; women nurtured amid the comforts and luxuries of their Eastern homes wept and prayed alternately, as their vision took in the waste of forests and the few acres of cleared, yet stumpy land, which environed their rude cabins.

However, all ended well for the Skinners, Athertons and most other members of the settlement, who, "with strong arms and undaunted hearts . . . wrought from the wilderness a competence and . . . the fruits of an honorable, industrious life in one of the most fertile regions of the state."

Jefferson Gage Thurber and Mary Bartlett Gerrish

A great desire to see Michigan opened up to railroad transportation

In 1833, an ambitious and classically educated lawyer — New Hampshire-born and New York-raised — headed for the Michigan frontier with a group of other young men.

The identity of his compatriots is now unknown, but Jefferson Gage Thurber left a big mark on his chosen community and chosen state.

Within a few years of his arrival in Monroe, he had become Monroe County prosecutor, then probate judge. He had also met and married Mary Bartlett Gerrish, another New Hampshire native.

Little more than a decade after he settled in Monore, Jefferson was elected to the state Senate. In 1851, he served as the Democratic speaker of the Michigan House of Representatives.

"He was a scholar. He was very widely read, in all things a very cultured man, unusually so for the Michigan frontier when

Jefferson Gage Thurber emigrated to Monroe as an ambitious young lawyer and became a political success, serving as both a state senator and as speaker of the Michigan House of Representatives. In the Senate, he chaired the Finance Committee and sat on the Committee on Internal Improvements. *Donald M. D. Thurber*

Mary Bartlett Gerrish Thurber. Mary Gerrish met and wed fellow New Hampshire native Jefferson Gage Thurber in Monroe. Although it is not known what attracted her to the frontier, she may have come to teach. She wrote to her parents in 1834 about the death by cholera of an acquaintance and said, "It will undoubtedly be a severe trial to her friends, yet their loss is not as great as many others. It seems as though all would be taken in Detroit. . . . All we can do is to stand prepared for what event shall be our lot." After her husband died in 1857, Mary returned to New Hampshire where she remarried. *Donald M. D. Thurber*

The Thurber house, shown about 1900, now is used by the Elks Club. In an 1834 letter to her parents in New Hampshire, Mary Thurber wrote, "You wished me to describe our house and furniture. I can give you but a very faint idea about it. There are five rooms below stairs, parlour, dining room, kitchen and two bed-rooms. The house is painted white with green blinds with three large cherry trees in front. The furniture of my parlour consists of a carpet table, a looking glass . . . not quite as large as yours, brass fire set, rocking chairs (they are called bamboo chairs) price $15. As to crockery, enough to be comfortable with, but not as much as I want." *Monroe County Historical Commission*

he moved there," said great-grandson Donald McDonald Dickinson Thurber.

Jefferson believed Monroe would become the railhead for southern Michigan. "It was already a port of sorts and had a natural harbor on Lake Erie," Donald Thurber said.

179

According to family tradition, Jefferson did not settle in Detroit because he believed Monroe to be "the coming metropolis of Michigan" and predicted that Detroit would "never amount to anything. It's too far from Monroe." Added Donald Thurber: "I'm sure he had a smile on his face when he said that."

In the Legislature, transportation proved to be Jefferson's main interest. "He had a great desire to see Michigan opened up to railroad transportation. I believe he did everything possible to encourage the building of railroads so Michigan would be well-served for markets," Donald said.

On the political front, he was an active Democrat who campaigned vigorously on behalf of Lewis Cass, the party's 1848 presidential candidate. Cass, Michigan's former territorial governor and U.S. senator, lost that hard-fought election to Zachary Taylor, a Whig.

One son continued the political tradition. Henry Thurber left his Detroit law practice in 1893 to become private secretary to President Grover Cleveland. The salary wasn't great, so Henry was asked if he could afford to accept the president's offer.

"Afford to go? There is nothing to be considered except Mr. Cleveland's call," he replied. "I would rather leave my children the record that he summoned me, that I accepted, and above all, that I in some measure fulfilled in his service his expectations of me, than to leave them a great fortune."

Peter Van Tifflin and Hannah Allen

Enjoying an extended acquaintance in all parts of the county

For Peter Van Tifflin's father Henry, involuntary service in Napoleon Bonaparte's army was an unattractive —and potentially deadly —prospect. Like many other Hollanders who were conscripted into Napoleon's army after the French invaded their country, Henry Van Tifflin looked for a way out.

"Napoleon had captured these people and they were forced to walk in front of his troops," Van Tifflin descendant Margaret Stelzer explained.

According to a family history, "When an expedition was sent to the West Indies and plans made to conquer the United States next, (Henry and some others) decided that they would no longer serve as cannon fodder to promote their leader's glory." Their alternative was desertion, followed by emigration to America.

Peter was only 8 years old when his family made its six-week

181

Van Tifflin family. Coming to America meant freedom from the threat of death in Napoleon's army for Henry Van Tifflin. Coming to Michigan meant hardships and opportunities for his son Peter. Their descendants David and Margaret Stelzer show pictures of their ancestors. *Charles Tines, The Detroit News*

voyage across the Atlantic. The Van Tifflins initially settled in a Dutch community in central New York.

Later, in the War of 1812, Peter joined an independent rifle company that fought against the British on Lake Ontario.

In 1833, he and a friend, John Remington, set off for the Michigan frontier in search of land to farm. He chose Grand

Esther Van Tifflin Howland and Henry H. Howland. New York-born Esther P. Van Tifflin, a daughter of Peter and Hannah Van Tifflin, married the widower Henry Howland and had five children. Howland was a prosperous farmer who originally worked on his father's Oakland County farm, then became one of the first settlers in Mundy Township, Genesee County. When he arrived, "it was then a wilderness, with but few inhabitants save its original owners, the Indians," a local history relates. "There was then no one within one mile of his land, and but 12 families in the town. His supplies were bought in Bloomfield, and five days were consumed in making the trip with an ox-team." *History of Genesee County, Michigan, 1879*

Blanc near Flint, and returned east for his wife Hannah Allen and their children. The family made the boat trip west by way of the Erie Canal and Lake Erie to Detroit in 1834.

"When he settled there he had to procure his flour and provisions at Detroit," according to a history of Genesee County. The

183

family lived in a log cabin until 1842, when Peter built a large frame house on the farm he had cleared.

"Our family, like all others, ate wild onions, plums, strawberries, blackberries and cranberries, as well as honey and nuts," the Van Tifflin history recounts. "There were no matches so they obtained fire from flint stones and for light burned cloths soaking in deer tallow."

The family made maple sugar, burned corn cobs to get soda, drank sage tea and used partridges rather than chickens for their meat pies. Flour was purchased from Rochester, salt pork came from Detroit, and groceries and other "necessities" were obtained in Pontiac, where the Van Tifflins sold their wool.

In his later years, Peter enjoyed attending county fairs and watching circus parades and square dances. He also liked to whittle hickory canes, read the Bible daily and listen as newspaper accounts of murders were read aloud.

As for the children of Hannah and Peter, son Reuben, a carpenter who helped build the county courthouse, was the successful bidder to construct a new school in Flint, "which contract was faithfully fulfilled to the entire satisfaction of the board of trustees, as expressed in a well-deserved resolution of commendation unanimously adopted." The project cost $77,377.

Daughter Esther married Henry H. Howland, a Mundy Township pioneer. Her brother William served as Mundy Township constable.

Andrew Ure and
Agnes Gardner

Roads were ruts and the river was the easiest route of transportation.

It was a long journey from a grocery shop in Glasgow, Scotland, to a pirate attack near the Madeira Islands off the northwest African coast.

It was a long journey from a well-drilling job in Halifax, Nova Scotia, to "assistant master" of a prison in Massachusetts.

And it was a long journey from Boston to Saginaw, when the area "was wild and wooded" and when "roads were ruts and the river was the easiest route of transportation."

Despite obvious hardships, Andrew Ure made those journeys and others.

Born in Scotland in 1778, Andrew gave up his job in a "mercantile establishment" to go to sea.

On his last voyage, he served as supercargo master on a sailing vessel that was captured during the French and Indian War. After pirates seized its cargo of wine and left the ship disabled, the crew mutinied. "With cutlasses," Andrew and the

The first Saginaw County courthouse was envisioned as an "orna-ment to the city, that it was expected would soon rise." Andrew Ure was recorded as one of "four public-spirited men who laid the plans for the building that served the county for nearly 50 years." Things didn't begin smoothly, however. In 1837, voters approved $10,000 in bonds to finance the project, but the original bids exceeded the money avail-able. Eventually, Asa Hill agreed to construct the courthouse for $9,510, but the State Bank of Saginaw proved unable to deliver the full $10,000. Construction was completed in 1843. *Historical Society of Saginaw County*

captain "drove the men below and stood guard over them for three days until they were picked up by a passing vessel," according to an account of the confrontation found by a descendant.

Because Andrew had lost his investment in the ill-fated voy-age, he emigrated to North America to make a new start. He settled first in Canada and then in Boston, where he met his wife-to-be, Scottish-born Agnes Gardner. In 1833, the couple and their children headed west.

Dissatisfied with what they found in Ohio and Kentucky, they decided to try Michigan, "attracted to Saginaw County by the glowing reports that other settlers made of the place," a county history said. "He was attracted to this portion of Michigan by the glowing reports of the wealth that was to be found in its timber resource."

Two years earlier, the French traveler and author Alexis de Tocqueville had visited the trading post where the city of Saginaw would develop. He predicted:

> In a few years these impenetrable forests will have fallen; the sons of civilization and industry will break the silence of the Saginaw; its echoes will cease; the banks will be imprisoned by quays, its current which now flows on unnoticed and tranquil through a nameless waste will be stemmed by the prows of vessels.

Agnes and the children waited three months in Detroit while Andrew bought land along the Tittabasassee River in Saginaw Township. The family initially lived in a log cabin at a time "when the pioneer settlers were few in number," and Agnes taught in a log school house. Later they built a frame house on their 250-acre farm.

Three years before Michigan attained statehood, territorial Gov. Stevens T. Mason appointed Andrew as an associate territorial judge, and he took an oath "to administer justice without respect to persons, and do equal right to the poor and to the sick."

Andrew helped make de Tocqueville's 1831 prophecy come true by assisting in the development of the city. He served as a Saginaw County commissioner, township supervisor and justice of the peace, and helped negotiate the loan that financed the first county courthouse. He was a Democrat until just before his death, when he allied himself with the Republicans.

Sons Robert and John Ure became active in local government as well, both serving as township supervisors. John became known for his "large and well-selected library," while Robert headed the county Republican party and ran unsuccessfully for the Legislature.

Timothy Horace Ives and Sophia Hale

In search of a distant Eden

When Chicago proved not to be the promised land, westward-bound Timothy Horace Ives reversed directions and doubled back eastward to Michigan.

It was 1834 when the New York native, his wife Sophia Hale and their children set out on that journey.

Timothy, the grandson of a Revolutionary War soldier, and Sophia believed that the plains of Illinois would be a "distant Eden." They sold their holdings in Pennsylvania for $3,000 in gold, loaded their belongings onto a Conestoga wagon and headed west. But they discovered Chicago to be "only a sea of mud with a few small shacks," according to a family account.

"They found Chicago in ruins from an Indian raid," explained great-great-granddaughter L. Pauline Irish. Disappointed, "they turned back in disgust" and spent an uncomfortable winter in South Bend, Ind., before discovering an ideal settlement spot overlooking the St. Joseph River in southern Berrien County.

Chief Leopold Pokagon. Pota-watomi Chief or Wkama – leader –Leopold Pokagon met Timothy and Sophia Ives during their first winter in Berrien County. A Chippewa by birth, he had been captured by the Potawatomi and married Sawak, the niece of Chief Topinabe. "Pokagon" means "rib" and, according to legend, that name was bestowed because he was wearing the rib of a slain enemy at the time of his capture. He was an influential leader in southwestern  Michigan, adjoining northern Indiana and the Chicago area and became the Kikowenine or designated official diplomatic speaker for a number of tribal villages. Because he had converted to Catholicism, he was able to protect his band from the wholesale expulsion and western relocation that devastated many other Eastern and Midwest tribes in the 1830s. As historian-anthropologist James A. Clifton wrote: "From 1828 on, Pokagon sought to transform his people in minimal ways that allowed them to remain in Michigan, avoiding removal westward, and to minimize disruption of their values and customs. . . . Acting for his people, he examined the future and found opportunity hidden amidst a thicket of adversity. He never lost his dignity, and he wedded ancient Potawatomi tradition to a setting of ceaseless change." *Northern Indiana Historical Society*

High on the bluff a splendid stand of walnut trees grew. Below the bluff, the river made a nearly complete circle.

"It reminded them so much of their home in Pennsylvania that they wanted it right away," Irish said. They set up camp and picked a site for their log cabin.

There was a problem, however: At the time, the land in what

Kalamazoo Land Office. Like thousands of other settlers, Timothy Ives purchased land from the federal government at this office in Kalamazoo. In the years before statehood, land offices were located in Detroit, Monroe, White Pigeon, Flint and Ionia. The White Pigeon office was relocated in 1834 to Kalamazoo, then known as Bronson. The general procedure was for prospective purchasers to obtain maps of available land and related surveyors' notes, then to travel or send a representative to examine the property, using a compass and maps to get there. Then they returned to the land office to make payment. Sale records were sent to Washington, and purchasers would later receive a presidentially-signed patent showing ownership. Land offices in Michigan sold more than 4 million acres in 1836 —literally doing a "land office business" —the most that year of any territory or state and in contrast with the 447,780 acres sold in 1833. The Kalamazoo office alone sold 1,634,500 acres in 1836, and was so busy that a tent city sprung up on empty Main Street lots to accommodate the crowds that poured in to buy land. *Robert Thom under commission from Michigan Bell*

eventually became the tiny community of Bertrand just north of the Indiana border was owned by the Potawatomis. The family history indicates that the local chief, Leopold Pokagon, demanded gifts to the tribe in exchange for the right to use their land.

"The gifts were almost all the foodstuffs they had acquired for the winter," Irish said, so the Ives survived that winter on parched corn and wild game. Timothy then "hied himself to Kalamazoo, where he filed his intention to buy the land they were living on" from the federal government.

Bertrand itself would boom and then bust. As a stop on the Chicago Road, it once boasted hotels and stores to service stage-coach passengers, but it declined after railroad routes bypassed the community.

Rufus Chancy Abbott and Malvina Tillottson

Just restless

Rufus Chancy Abbott was a hard man to pin down, a man rooted in his family rather than in any particular place.

A log of his 52 years would register his birth in eastern New York, his marriage in central New York, a move to what is now Southfield in Michigan Territory, his resettlement in Allegan County, a return to New York, a move to Pennsylvania, another move to New York and his death in Indiana.

Chancy, as he was called, and his wife Malvina Tillottson had 10 children born in three states.

"I guess they were just restless," said Kenneth L. Abbott, their great grandson. "Back then you could get land pretty cheaply. A lot of families traveled in that era."

The couple came to Michigan in 1835, then bought 40 acres in what became Gun Plain Township, Allegan County, where records show their 1837–1838 school taxes totalled $1.28. Chancy was elected township tax collector and highway com-

Malvina Tillottson Abbott. With her husband Rufus Chancy Abbott, Malvina led a nomadic life between New York, Michigan, Pennsylvania and Indiana. She outlived her husband by half a century and, at age 95, died at the Ohio home of her youngest daughter in 1904. *Kenneth L. Abbott*

missioner, making it appear for a while that the Abbotts were settling down for good. It was not to be.

"Though the family seemed to be doing well, they returned to New York" sometime during 1841 or 1842, according to an historical account. Their farm was sold in 1848.

Back east, the 1850 census listed Chancy's occupation as a boatman on the Erie Canal. A Michigan-born son, Chancy Jr., would later remember taking canal trips with his "captain father."

Chancy Jr., a carpenter by trade, carried his own touch of restlessness. Early in 1861 at Burr Oak, he enlisted as a private in the 6th Michigan Infantry and was mustered out in Detroit a few months later. He married in Indiana, had his first baby in Missouri and spent the last part of his life back in Indiana. A "quiet unassuming man, highly respected," he was known as "a great reader and a close observer and was well posted on all subjects," according to one account.

Abbott Barn. This barn was built on the Gun Plain Township farm of Rufus and Malvina Abbott. They left this farm in the early 1840s to return to their home state of New York. As an Allegan County history explained, "All who came to Michigan in those days did not remain. Many who started out from the Empire State with buoyant hopes, flushed with the anticipation of cheap homes and a future competency in the new state, became utterly discouraged by the privations they have endured." *Kenneth L. Abbott*

"The story goes that he was going west and got as far west as Chicago and decided he didn't want to continue, so he turned around and came back," Kenneth Abbott said.

195

Dexter Arnold and Olive Kimball

Conflict in the classroom

Ionia was a remote 2-year-old outpost of four log homes and a single frame house when Dexter Arnold and his wife Olive Kimball arrived in the fall of 1835, accompanied by their 8-year-old son William.

Dexter, a Revolutionary War descendant, cleared some space in the woods to build a log cabin. The following year, the family moved a mile north of the tiny settlement to start a new farm.

Dexter became involved in a heated controversy with Thomas Chamberlain, a local teacher described by an Ionia County history as a "small man but a strict disciplinarian." As one of Chamberlain's strongest and most vocal critics, Dexter attended a school meeting where the discipline issue was to be argued.

"At the meeting, Arnold grew somewhat excited and charged Chamberlain with being a bulldog, only to bite and hang on, to which Chamberlain publicly answered him: 'Yes I am, and you

Dexter Arnold. As a settler in frontier Ionia County, Dexter Arnold sparked a community controversy when he instigated a school meeting to challenge the teacher's "severity" toward the pupils, including his sons. The majority of parents "strongly sustained and indorsed him as a capable and correct teacher, and dismissed the charges." *Stella Chase*

can't shake me off either.'" The majority sided with the teacher on the issue, "much to Arnold's chagrin and the corresponding triumph of the pedagogue."

In 1855, son William set out on his own, building a log cabin and farm five miles away on 160 acres of land in Easton Township. He was considered "a good farmer and an active and energetic citizen who early became regarded as one of the leaders in the community life in his neighborhood," the county history says. His cabin was replaced by a frame house that later would be expanded into a "commodious residence." William became a steward of the local Wesleyan Methodist Church. Both he and his wife Isabel Kimball were active prohibitionists, and Isabel served as treasurer of the local Woman's Christian Temperance Union.

William and Isabel Arnold. William Arnold came from New York to Ionia County as a child, later earning a reputation as a good farmer and community leader. He became Easton Township supervisor. Isabel Kimball, his Virginia-born wife, was treasurer of the Woman's Christian Temperance Union. The couple was "in full sympathy with all movements designed to advance the general welfare of their community." *History of Ionia County, Michigan, 1916*

Jehudi Ashmun and Nancy Adeline Morley

Wrought at his trade as a ship carpenter

There was little need for Jehudi Ashmun's shipbuilding skills when he worked as a farmer in Oakland County. but the New York native went on to establish the first shipyard on the Saginaw River.

Born in 1809, he was a child when his parents moved to Ontario where he learned the ship carpenter trade. At the age of 26, he moved with his parents to what was described as a "wild bush farm" in Milford Township.

It was there that he met Nancy Adeline Morley, who lived a few miles away in Lyon Township. Nancy, the daughter of a War of 1812 soldier, had arrived in Michigan Territory as a young girl.

A justice of the peace performed the marriage ceremony, and the couple lived on their Oakland County farm for a decade and a half until 1852, when they decided to head north.

In Saginaw, Jehudi "wrought at his trade as a ship carpenter,

Jehudi and Nancy Ashmun. Jehudi Ashmun became the first ship-builder on the Saginaw River after he gave up farming in Oakland County and moved north. Nancy was a temperance activist. *Ruby Templeton*

building the first sailing crafts ever built on the Saginaw River," according to an historical account. Nancy became one of the original members of Epworth Methodist Episcopal Church and was active in the anti-liquor temperance movement.

During Jehudi's 30 years on the south side of Saginaw, the city was transformed from a "rude hamlet of shanties, planted on the edge of a swamp to be the presentable and industrious city," the account said. "The years passed by, and from the swampy morass gradually grew and expanded the beautiful city he had beheld the first inception of," another account said.

At Jehudi's death in 1882, a newspaper eulogized him as one of a shrinking number of early settlers, saying, "So falls the stately cedars one by one, and their place is occupied by a new generation, who reap where their predecessors have sown and gather today in joy the fruits planted in privation."

When Nancy died a few years later, she too was mourned as one of the early arrivals on the frontier. "The pioneers of Saginaw are rapidly passing away," it was observed.

Joseph William Lawrence Sr. and Sybil Heath

Potatoes frozen hard as flints

Hard times back east lured blacksmiths Joseph William Lawrence Sr. and his son, Joseph Jr., to Michigan.

"Business was bad. They had a big depression so they decided to pack up and head west," descendant Charles Henry Lawrence explained.

It was 1835 when three generations of Lawrences made an exploratory foray from New York into remote Branch County, just north of the Indiana border. At that time, Joseph Jr.'s son James "cut the first tree and rolled up the logs for the first shelter of settlers," according to an historical account. That date: his 21st birthday.

More than 50 years later, James wrote about that day: "We had to make in that short wintry afternoon a shelter for our luckless heads from the wild winter storm that threatened to burst upon us before night." The Lawrences and their companions quickly built a house "three logs high," and "our fire soon

202

Joseph William Lawrence Jr.
With his father and son, Joseph W. Lawrence Jr. scouted out southern Michigan in 1835 as a potential new home for their financially hard-pressed family. His son James later described that exploratory winter journey as a time of hardship, with bread "as tough as one of our oak shingles" and potatoes "frozen hard as flints." *Charles Henry Lawrence*

gave a cheerful light, lighting up the surrounding darkness, and we were busy cooking our rations of salt pork on the coals and on forked sticks."

Their diet was far from luxurious: "Our daily fare was bread, meat and potatoes, with salt. Our potatoes were frozen hard as flints the first night we came, and to keep them carefully we threw them down outside the house on the ground. Our bread was strictly and literally home made, of salt and flour, wet with cold water and baked in our frying pan before the fire, and when done it was solid and substantial, and about as tough as one of our oak shingles."

In 1836, the Lawrences recorded claims with the U.S. Land Office and the next year moved their families permanently to Michigan.

History records how Joseph Sr. cut his "final ties to friends and associates of more than 40 years, and at the age of 66 set out to contend with the privations of pioneer life in Michigan." Traveling with them were Joseph Sr.'s wife Sybil Health, Joseph Jr.'s wife Susan North, and their children.

Joseph Sr. traveled with a light one-horse wagon "covered above and carpeted within," while Joseph Jr. transported his family in a new two-horse wagon with a canvas cover. They found themselves far from stage routes and 16 miles from the nearest post office.

Just as the organization of Michigan underwent rapid changes immediately before and after statehood, southeastern Branch County changed as well. When the Lawrences first arrived, the land they farmed was part of Coldwater Township. A year later, it was put into Quincy Township and later into Algansee Township before California Township was organized in 1846.

Joseph Sr. became California Township's original elections inspector at a schoolhouse meeting. At the same session, officials adopted a $5 bounty for any "full-grown wolf or bear caught and killed in this town" and voted against granting a license to sell "intoxicating liquors for the ensuing year."

Joseph Jr. later served as justice of the peace. And James, that first tree-cutter and chronicler of the expedition, became township highway commissioner.

Isaac Truax and Angelica DeLa Grange

Endured great hardships that he might give them prosperity

Nobody could accuse Isaac Truax of living a life of luxury when he brought his growing family to Brandon Township in northern Oakland County.

Their first home in 1835 was a cave-like shanty covered with elm bark and built into the side of a hill. Their only income came from trapping wolves and collecting the $5 bounty on each. On one occasion, Isaac kept a pregnant wolf until she gave birth, increasing the amount of money he could claim. The bounties paid for their first cow, among other necessities, and the original shanty was replaced by a log home.

Isaac was both a glassblower and a farmer, and he traveled to Detroit and Pontiac to trade. He carried corn meal on his back 20 miles to feed his wife Angelica DeLa Grange and their children.

What was Brandon Township like in those days?

The environment was hostile: "A vast wilderness inhabited by Indians, wolves, deer and bear," according to the description in a 19th century Oakland County history. And the area where the family settled was isolated, "the scarcity of roads rendering communication very difficult."

Isaac initially explored Michigan with his son Isaac C. and daughter Maria. Pleased with what they saw, they returned east to collect the rest of the family, who traveled to the frontier by way of the Erie Canal, a steamer to Detroit and a horse team to Brandon Township. In Michigan, they had seven more children.

Isaac and Angelica bought 80 acres for farming, and their deed was signed by President Andrew Jackson. Two years later, Jackson would sign the act of Congress admitting Michigan to the Union.

Isaac "endured great hardships that he might give them prosperity in the future," the history relates. Perhaps what he had learned from his father, a Revolutionary War veteran who had pioneered in western New York, helped him cope with those hardships.

According to another description, "In this part of the township game was very plenty, especially deer, and venison was the principal meat of the settlers. It was customary to carry along the rifle, even to religious meetings."

Although his father had been a renowned hunter, hunting skills proved not to be among Isaac's own attributes. Family history recounts how he "would shoot the deer in the body and they would run away, and he would come back home without any venison." One day when he returned empty-handed and disgusted, he handed the rifle to his son Isaac C., who soon spotted a buck and killed it with a single shot. The son then became the family's chief meat-gatherer.

Maria was known for fortitude, endurance and ability to meet challenges. One winter, she walked 20 miles to Pontiac, where she bought a rocking chair and started to carry it back to the farm. Her brother found Maria resting in the rocker along the trail near their home.

William Van Blarcom and Mary Palmatier

Among thieves on the Chicago Road

It was the fall of 1835 when William Van Blarcom and his son Joseph ventured with a "single horse and light wagon" from New York to seek a new life in Michigan.

Their journey through Canada and Detroit was not easy. Before reaching their goal, they fell among thieves along the Chicago Road near the border of Hillsdale and Branch counties at an inn owned by a man named Osborn.

A strongbox strapped to the back of their wagon was stolen. In it, according to one historical account, was a "major portion" of Joseph's "earthly possessions," including his clothes. After the theft, William and Joseph spent several days hunting for their missing goods.

"The landlord tendered his sympathy and apparently was much concerned and interested in hunting up those who had committed the robbery upon his premises." He blamed other emigrants from the East who had "encamped in the vicinity

Joseph and Luceba Van Blarcom. Joseph Van Blarcom came to Michigan in 1835 in search of farmland and settled in Branch County the next year. With him is his wife Luceba Worden. *Thomas H. Brockway*

during the nighttime," a Branch County history explained. "But nothing resulted other than to swell their expenses at the (inn) of the rascal who perpetrated the robbery himself."

Although there are some contradictions among the accounts of the Van Blarcoms' exploratory trip to Michigan, one book relates that expenses for totalled $14.42. That cost was higher than expected due to the theft.

Despite the losses, they were in better shape than many other pioneers because they still had a horse.

Undeterred by the theft, William and Joseph continued to Girard Township in Branch County, where they found land suitable for settlement. William returned east to retrieve his wife

Along the Chicago Road. William and Joseph Van Blarcom traveled across southern Michigan along the Chicago Road (*preceding page*), which closely followed the Sauk trail. Parts of the road were unimproved and uncomfortable, and it was described as "a huge serpent lazily pursuing its onward course, utterly unconcerned as to its destination." Originally surveyed in 1825 as a military route between forts in Detroit and Chicago, it soon became a highway for settlers. By 1835, the Western Stage Co. of Detroit was running two stages daily along the route, and a stagecoach could travel the distance in 4½ days. This mural, painted by Roy C. Gamble for the 1933 Chicago World's Fair, depicts Native Americans watching as pioneers stream westward on the Chicago Road, inevitably and permanently changing the face of Michigan Territory. *Michigan Bureau of History*

Mary Palmatier and their three other sons, and the family moved permanently to Michigan in 1836.

William became a member of the township election board that oversaw the vote on statehood. He and Joseph are believed to have been farmers and land speculators and also may have operated a mill or sawmill. Census reports at various times also listed William as a merchant, as blind and as unable to read or write.

William Witherspoon and Johanna Hayes

From baker to soldier

Far from his native Scotland, William Witherspoon gave his life while serving an adopted land split by bitter rivalries:

It was 1834 when the 17-year-old youth left Europe, settling in Detroit the following year.

And it was 1863 when William, a first sergeant in Company C of the 27th Michigan Infantry Regiment, came down with a fatal case of "congestion of the lungs" —pneumonia — during winter regimental maneuvers far from the southern battlefields.

The nearly three decades between his immigration to Michigan and his death had been busy and successful.

Upon his arrival in Detroit, the young man made a living as a baker. There in the growing city, William met another Scotland-born immigrant, Johanna Hayes. Their marriage, like Michigan's statehood, occurred in 1837.

As his business prospered, William purchased land along the Detroit River and engaged in land transactions with a younger man destined to become his son-in-law. That associate, Alexander Witherspoon, coincidentally had the same last name although the two families were not related.

When the Civil War broke out, William rushed to enlist in the Union Army. His new son-in-law also enlisted, as did Alexander's brothers, John and George.

A letter from William's lieutenant detailed how he became deathly ill: It was extremely cold one February day in 1863 when the regiment moved from its rendezvous at Port Huron to Ypsilanti. William, "being much exposed, contracted the disease," the lieutenant wrote. He died at home while on furlough two months after winning a promotion to first sergeant.

After the war, son-in-law Alexander became a U.S. Customs officer in Detroit. Several children from his marriage to William's oldest daughter Joanna became active in local politics.

Josiah W. Begole and Harriet A. Miles

Broad nature and sterling qualities

There were headlines when the would-be governor switched political parties.

It was more than a century ago when Josiah W. Begole converted from the Republican Party —which he had joined when it was founded in 1854 in Jackson —to the Greenback Party and eventually to the Democrats.

The conversion made him governor on a Greenback-Democratic fusion ticket in 1883, 47 years after he moved from western New York, eventually to settle in the tiny five-house hamlet of Flint.

Born 12 days after the Battle of New Orleans, Begole was descended from Maryland slave owners who became Abolitionists and moved to New York, where they freed their own slaves. The eldest of 10 children, he was educated in a log schoolhouse.

In 1836, the 21-year-old Josiah set out for Michigan with $100

Josiah W. Begole. Political and business achievements made Josiah Begole a success, but not without hard work on the frontier. "Being the eldest of a family of 10 children, he was early taught habits of industry, and when 21 years of age he left the parental roof to seek a home in the Territory of Michigan, then an almost unbroken wilderness," a biographical sketch relates. "Immediately after his marriage he commenced work on an unimproved farm, where by his perseverance and energy, he soon established a good home, and at the end of 18 years was the owner of a farm of 500 acres well improved." *State Archives of Michigan*

Harriet A. Begole. When Harriet Begole's eldest son William was wounded in the Civil War, she rushed to nurse him, using a pass from an Army general to secure a seat aboard a train headed to Georgia with reinforcements for the front. "There was not another woman on board. She stayed four weary weeks with her son till death ended his sufferings. Then she brought his body home," daughter Mary Begole Cummings later wrote. When another son was stricken with typhoid in Cincinnati, Harriet traveled there too, and "the attending physician told her that dozens of his patients were dying for lack of such care as she gave her son." *State Archives of Michigan*

214

The Begole home. Josiah and Harriet Miles built this home in Flint, where Josiah remained active after his unsuccessful campaign for a second term as governor. In an 1882 address, he recalled life in a log cabin and expressed mixed feelings about the grandeur of homes such as this one: "It is pleasant to have a house of eight or 10 rooms, with its appropriate furniture and adornments, but we very much doubt whether these things make us more happy, or contribute greatly to our family and social enjoyment." *History of Genesee County, Michigan, 1879*

in savings, traveling by steamer to Toledo and from there to Jackson and on to Flint by foot.

"His life parallels the history of Flint," said Harriet DeCamp Lay, his great-great-great granddaughter. When he arrived in Flint, he worked as a teacher and bought 80 acres of land for farming, eventually expanding his holdings to 500 acres. When timbering prospered, he owned a lumber company. And when wagon-making became important to the city, he owned a wagon works firm.

Once the Civil War broke out, "he took an active part in recruiting, furnishing supplies to the army and looking after the interests of solders' families," a Genesee County history relates. His eldest son was killed in the war near Atlanta.

As what one biographer called "an anti-slavery man," Josiah had joined the Republican party at its inception. He eventually held local offices, was elected to the state Senate and served a term in Congress.

His wife Harriet A. Miles helped found the city's first subscription library and accompanied Josiah to Washington and Lansing when his official duties called him there.

Josiah switched to the Greenback Party, which advocated the issuance of large amounts of paper money and was especially popular among farmers. The party, active between 1876 and 1884, also favored women's suffrage, an eight-hour work day and an income tax.

He was elected governor, "one of the few men to successfully upset the two-party system," Lay said. That victory, she explained, was more personal than political because teetotalers abandoned his Republican opponent, incumbent Gov. David H. Jerome, who was rumored to have "flirted with demon rum."

During his two-year tenure in Lansing as governor in 1883–1884, Josiah was interested in the rights of criminals. His inaugural address called for abolition of the contract labor system in which the state provided inmates to private businesses. He established Michigan's first criminal insane asylum, as well as the Bureau of Labor Statistics. But perhaps ironically for one who had come to Michigan as a pioneer himself, he favored closing the state immigration office which was successfully bringing Europeans to Michigan.

After a narrow reelection defeat by Republican Civil War hero Russell A. Alger, he remained active in business, community and church affairs until his death in 1896.

216

A newspaper obituary lauded him as "a man of broad nature and sterling qualities of both mind and heart." He was, the paper reported, "self-made" and "never failing to respond to the calls of charity or the cry of the distressed." And his efforts on the frontier were not forgotten when Gov. John T. Rich eulogized him as "one of those who who helped redeem our state from a wilderness."

As Josiah Begole wrote in 1881 when a shipment of relief supplies to forest fire victims in the Thumb was delayed, "Draw on me . . . . Let no one suffer while I have money."

Henry Birge and Sarah Staples

One of the patriarchs of Oakland County

For Henry Birge, Michigan meant opportunity — and a lot of moving around.

During more than six decades in the territory and the newborn state, the Pennsylvania native lived in several Oakland County communities as well as Lansing and tried his hand at various occupations. Henry arrived in Waterford Township in 1836, working at a local sawmill and on a farm. He also bought property in Ingham, Clinton and Jackson counties, according to land records.

The travel bug apparently bit again in 1837, when Henry and two older brothers headed for Wisconsin. Henry decided that he preferred Michigan after all, however, and returned in 1838.

That year he married New York-born Sarah Staples, a descendant of Revolutionary War participants. The young couple started saving money to buy their own property in Pontiac.

Then in 1848, it was north to Lansing, where Henry became

proprietor of a livery. "Not finding the occupation congenial, he sold out the business" and purchased a farm in Waterford Township, an Oakland County history reports.

After two years, the Birges moved to West Bloomfield, then 10 months later bought another Waterford farm.

There Henry stayed and prospered, becoming what was characterized as an "influential and well-to-do citizen." Henry, it was written, owned "substantial outbuildings, good machinery and everything convenient for carrying on farming." Another report noted that "he has done general farming in a sensible, practical way, and has been particularly successful in raising sheep, cattle and horses, taking prizes for his fine Durham cattle and Southdown sheep."

The children of Sarah and Henry "all received good common school educations" and one son spent two years in high school — an unusual accomplishment in frontier times. Their daughter Fannie married a wealth Lapeer County lumber dealer and farmer. And Fannie's son became a respected physician in the Thumb, where he died of pneumonia contracted while making house calls by horse and buggy.

History even kept track of Henry's political orientation: His first vote was for Martin Van Buren and "he has never failed on any account to cast his vote for every Democratic candidate for president since."

Sarah died in Drayton Plains in 1896. Henry survived until 1912, and before his death was described as "one of the patriarchs of Oakland County, where he has witnessed wonderful developments and has taken an honorable part in its growth and progress."

Japheth Fisher and Maria Williams

A notch at a time

Tough? What's tough?

Getting lost in the wilderness but —undaunted —persevering to start the first farm in an unsettled township.

Building a barn alone, carrying the heavy logs up a ladder "a notch at a time and laying them properly in their places."

Walking barefoot to frontier logging bees "where great savage thistles are apt to abound," then laughing when friends push you onto "the fangs of those thistles."

That's tough.

So was Japheth Fisher, the first resident of Benton Township in Eaton County. The Vermont-born descendant of an old New England family arrived in Michigan in 1836 from New York, where he had worked on the docks of New York City and along the Erie Canal.

He spent his first Michigan winter timbering in Allegan County, where he helped build a mill. From his $266 earnings, he paid $49.75 for a barrel of flour and half a barrel of pork, using the rest of the money to buy 80 acres of virgin forest near what would become Charlotte.

In the summer of 1837, he began the tough task of claiming a farm from the woods and raising corn and potatoes. His first house there was an 8-by-10-foot trough-roofed shanty. The following year, he married another Vermont transplant, Maria Williams, who lived in neighboring Chester Township.

When Maria was ready to give birth to their first child, she returned to her mother's house because the Fishers had no neighbors to assist her. The next eight children were born in their own home though.

Japheth and Maria planted the first orchard and operated the first brick-making business and cider press in the county. They also donated land on their farm for construction of a frame schoolhouse that Japheth built with the help of two neighbors.

Larned Gore and Lucinda Bonney

Filled with wanderlust

You need a map to keep tabs on Larned Gore and his sons, Albert and Mahlon —roamers all.

Born in Pennsylvania in 1809, Larned was married in New York, moved to Ohio and then settled in the western part of Michigan Territory in 1836.

That odyssey, impressive enough for early 19th-century America, proved to be a mere prelude to the more extensive travels of his boys, however.

But first, let's back up to Larned's arrival in Michigan.

It was the year before statehood when he and his wife Lucinda Bonney bought 120 acres of government land in West Leroy, south of Battle Creek in Calhoun County. Albert and Mahlon were children at the time. Larned built a barn of hand-hewn logs held together by wooden pegs and earned a reputation as a hard-working and successful farmer.

Mahlon ran away from home at age 15 to learn the printing

Larned & Lucinda Gore. In 1836, Larned and Lucinda Gore settled south of Battle Creek after living in Ohio and New York. *Eleanor M. Boston*

Mahlon Gore. The peripatetic Mahlon Gore came to Michigan as a child and later served in the South Dakota legislature. A printer by trade, he published newspapers in three states and was elected mayor of Orlando, Fla. *South Dakota State Historical Society*

Albert and Candace Gore. Civil War veteran Albert Gore traveled to South Dakota with his wife Candace, became a Missouri newspaper publisher and eventually settled in California. *Eleanor M. Boston*

trade at the *Marshall Statesman*. Albert graduated from Baptist College in Kalamazoo.

When the Civil War erupted, Albert was quick to enlist in the Union cause. Honorably discharged in 1862 with the rank of first lieutenant, Albert returned to Michigan but he and Mahlon packed up their families and headed by train to Iowa.

From there it was west by covered wagon to the Dakota Territory, where the brothers went into politics and helped South Dakota attain statehood. Both served in the new legislature there and Albert, who was an ordained minister, worked as a missionary.

But the urge to roam persisted. Albert returned to Michigan

224

in 1865, re-enlisted in the Army and served with the 1st Michigan Sharpshooters and an Illinois unit.

Two years after the war ended, Albert relocated again, this time to Independence, Mo., where he published a newspaper. From Missouri, it was back to Michigan in 1875. Then faced with health problems in 1880, he headed to California where he lived another 40 years.

As for Mahlon, the other roving brother, he published newspapers in South Dakota, Iowa and Florida and served two years as mayor of Orlando.

John Herman Hanses and Elizabeth Martin

Immeasurable comfort in their faith

John Herman Hanses spoke no English when he helped establish the Clinton County community of Westphalia in November 1836.

The 40-year-old farmer's son and his companions had sailed from Bremen in their German homeland in August that year, landed in New York in October and left the East by way of the Erie Canal the same month.

"They very likely had suffered the pangs of homesickness, privation and poverty long before they reached Detroit," a history of Westphalia's St. Mary's Roman Catholic parish says. "They were not even acquainted with the language of their adopted country and it can be imagined how utterly lost they must have felt in this strange land."

John was unmarried at the time, but his four companions — William Tillmann, John Salter, Anton Cordes and Joseph Platte

—left their families in Detroit and headed northward to find a suitable spot for their settlement.

Father Anton Kopp, also born in Westphalia, Germany, recommended the Grand River valley as a potential site. The party hired William Hunt, a fur trapper and trader, to guide them to newly surveyed but still unsettled land there. Once they arrived, John used the inheritance he had brought in gold coins to buy 136 acres.

Together with Kopp —known as the "Pioneer Priest" —the companions founded the village of Westphalia northwest of the future city of Lansing. It was named in honor of their distant homeland.

Land was cheap at $1 an acre but food was scarce and expensive during their first summer on the frontier. They worked with primitive tools, and their rough cabins had no doors or windows. "It was some time before a team of oxen was brought to Westphalia and the back of the pioneer was sorely tried in the work of clearing and tilling the land," according to a local account. John once recalled how the mid-Michigan forest was so thick that the men had to chop down a tree to see the sky.

Historian F. Clever Bald wrote that John Hanses and his companions faced a tougher challenge than other German immigrants of the time: "Their struggle to make a home in the wilderness was more difficult than that of their fellow countrymen for the Westphalians were very poor, and the land that they acquired was practically cut off from the settled parts of the state."

Despite its remoteness, Michigan's second early German settlement had grown to 22 families by 1838.

Charles F. Loeher related a traditional family tale about how John, his great-great grandfather, used a hand sled to drag heavy barrels of flour the 10 miles from Portland in Ionia County. He was forced to stop every few minutes to lift the barrels over fallen trees that blocked the way.

John's status as the community's pioneer bachelor lasted but a

Founders of Westphalia. John Hanses, Father Anton Kopp and four other German immigrants founded both the community of Westphalia and St. Mary's Roman Catholic Church in 1836. This painting (*opposite*) by G. Zamboni was commissioned to symbolically portray both events for their centennial commemorations. *Westphalia Historical Society*

few years. When he fell seriously ill with a fever, a neighbor's daughter, German-born Elizabeth Martin, took care of him. They were married in a "humble wedding feast" in 1840, with Kopp officiating.

As a history of Westphalia put it, "Imagine the courage of these early immigrants in striking out as they did in a strange wild country to find future homes for themselves. As strangers in a strange land they found immeasurable comfort in their faith."

Father Anton Kopp, a founder of Westphalia, was known as the "Pioneer Priest" for his work on the frontier among fellow German Catholics such as Elizabeth Martin and John Hanses. He celebrated mass in the settlers' homes until a modest log church was built in 1838. It was said of Kopp, "He was not only a pastor but a practical organizer. He understood the problems of his growing parish." *Westphalia Historical Society*

229

William C. Leek and Martha Willey

Planted apple seeds from the East

Martha Willey Leek never harvested Johnny Appleseed's fame but the New Hampshire-born woman made sure apples blossomed at her new home in the Michigan wilderness.

"She burned off a brush heap and planted apple seeds that she had brought with her from the East," a history of Ingham County relates.

In 1836 or 1837, Martha and her husband William C. Leek became early settlers in Alaiedon Township.

The Leeks left New York, then made their way from Ohio to Michigan by ox cart. They were forced to cut a road through the forest to complete the final seven miles of their trek.

Once they arrived at the lakeside property they intended to farm, the wagon was unloaded, turned upside down and raised on posts to shelter the family until a house could be built.

William was elected justice of the peace at the township's first meeting in the newly platted village of Jefferson City. Some local

Leek tombstone and cemetery. Like many early settlers, William and Martha Leek provided land from their recently acquired property for a community cemetery. Many pioneer burial grounds have been abandoned and overgrown, but the Leek Cemetery is still in use. William's tombstone shows that he died June 20, 1852, at the age of 59 years, eight months and 12 days. *Eric Freedman*

residents hoped the community would become the state capital —or at least the county seat —and visitor Silas Beebe predicted that it "will undoubtedly be a place of some importance some-day, being the center of the county and nearly of the state." Nearby Mason would never amount to much, Beebe forecast.

That was not to be —the railroad bypassed Jefferson City, and so did history. Ironically, rival Mason was chosen as the seat of the county which would host the capital city. And Jefferson City disappeared from the map.

Like many other pioneers across Michigan, the Leeks made land available for community use. They sold a plot to the town-ship for a "burying ground" and leased nearby land to what would be called the Leek School District. The teacher was "boarded around" among the families and paid $1 a week until 1846, when the weekly salary rose to $1.25.

"Mr. Leek by ceding land to the people for school and burial purposes unwittingly made his name imperishable," according to the county history. Probably more important to Martha, how-ever, was the fact that children at the school were able to pick and enjoy apples during recess.

Martha's appleseed planting efforts never became the stuff of folk legends, but lack of public recognition was not unusual in the wilderness.

As a 19th century account put it: "No resident of the Leek district has ever achieved national renown, and none have landed in prison, or in politics, and it is a comfort to reflect on the saying of Abraham Lincoln that 'the Lord must have loved the common folks, he made so many of them.'"

William became known as a "master farmer" and Martha's apple seeds remained a legacy. As their eldest granddaughter once wrote, "I well remember a few of those trees with most delicious apples."

Nathan E. Lewis and Catherine Ann Lopeman

Soldiers, father and son

For father and son, the Civil War meant a long time away from home.

Connecticut native Nathan E. Lewis, who had settled in northwest Macomb County more than two decades earlier, spent three years in battle with the 7th and 10th Michigan Infantry.

Meanwhile, Michigan-born son Josiah fought in the 4th Michigan Cavalry.

After the war, Nathan spent the rest of his life in Lapeer County with his wife Catherine Ann Lopeman. Josiah, a year after his discharge, married Minerva Jane Pease and began to move around the eastern part of the state.

It's unlikely that Michigan had been Nathan's intended destination in 1815 when, at the age of 8, his father took the family from Connecticut to Pennsylvania. Four years later they relocated to Ohio.

In 1836, Nathan moved again, this time to Bruce Township in Macomb County, and a little later headed a short distance north into Lapeer County's Dryden Township.

The hazards of military duty took a lifelong toll on Josiah. One history gives this account of what happened to him while fighting in Tennessee:

"In the battle of Stone River, his horse's head was shot off, and he was wounded at the battle of Shelbyville below the left knee in a saber charge, which has made him a cripple for life." He walked with a cane until his death.

The war injury did not prevent Josiah from public service, however. In 1873, he and Minerva moved to Sanilac County on Lake Huron, where he was elected Sanilac Township clerk.

The couple later left for Tuscola County, where he became Novesta Township clerk and then supervisor.

"When he first came to the township, he had few neighbors, no roads or clearing on his place. His first work was to build a shanty, which he covered with boards and shakes and which had no doors or windows," according to a history of Tuscola County. "He assessed the township that year and had to buy a pair of rubber boots to wade through the water to accomplish his work."

In his obituary, he was remembered as a "man of large heart. If 'Uncle Joe' met a fellow creature who was 'down and out,' the unfortunate could count on a friend."

Adam Manwaring and Susan Platt

A man of strictest integrity

George Washington never made it to Michigan, and most residents of the territory never saw the proverbial father of their country.

Adam Manwaring was an exception.

Born at the end of the Revolutionary War ended, Adam was a child in his native New Jersey when Washington came to town.

It was many years later that he and his wife Susan Platt decided to come west. They initially settled in what was then Avon Township, Oakland County, in 1836 and soon afterward bought 160 acres of land in Lapeer County's Dryden Township.

Grandson George Manwaring later described Adam as a short man with long gray whiskers —"you could hardly see his face for the whiskers" —who read the Bible to the family each evening. George recorded in that Bible how "I remember seeing

Joshua Manwaring was twice elected to the Michigan Senate as a Democrat. When he arrived in Michigan Territory with his family, he "worked on the farm summers, attending the district school winters, and by dint of hard study acquired a good business education," according to a Lapeer County history. He put that education to work over the years in the sawmill and "mercantile" businesses, and it was said, "Go to Manwaring's Mill and you can get anything you want." In Lansing, he chaired the Senate Committee for the Deaf and Dumb and sat on committees dealing with lumbering and the state agricultural college in East Lansing, now Michigan State University. *State Archives of Michigan*

lots of flint gun locks which he had taken from guns and changed them to percussion locks."

The marriage of Adam and Susan produced 15 children. One son, Joseph, served a term in the Michigan House of Representatives and spent a number of years as township supervisor and clerk. Another son, Joshua, spent two terms in the state Senate. The brothers' legislative tenures overlapped, although Joshua was a Democrat and Joseph was a Republican.

Family history records that Adam voted in every presidential election from Thomas Jefferson's until 1874, when he died at age 92.

At his death, the *Pontiac Gazette* characterized him as a "kind

Old Manwaring pharmacy. A Greek Revival building originally used by Joseph and Ella Manwaring for their pharmacy was moved from Dryden to the Genesee Recreation Area near Flint and restored. It now serves as the print shop at Crossroads Villiage, a "living village" of 19th century life. *Genesee County Parks & Recreation Commission*

and indulgent father" who was "held in high estimation as a man of the strictest integrity and of unimpeachable character."

Joseph and his wife Ella were among the state's first pharmacists, operating their pharmacy until 1907. The Dryden post office was also located in their store for 23 years. Ella was among the founders of the Ladies Library Association, set up to provide reading material to the community at little cost. The couple raised a Dryden-born orphan, George Owen Squier, who became a renowned inventor, the first passenger on Orville Wright's test flights of army aircraft and chief of the Army Air Service in World War I.

237

Jared Sanford Rogers and Louisa Miller

Into the "dense wilderness"

The heavy westward migration of 1836 brought thousands of settlers, including the family of Jared Sanford Rogers, to Michigan Territory —hungry for cheap but fertile farm land and willing to wrest it from the wilderness of prairies and forests.

The Rogers made the difficult journey west accompanied by the families of two New York neighbors, J.S. Henyon and E. R. Carpenter.

When they arrived in Barry County, their children and wives waited at the Bunker Tavern in Hastings while the three men cleared a road and built log cabins on land they bought for $1.25 an acre in the "dense wilderness" of Carlton Township.

Jared and his wife Louisa Miller became active in their new community. Louisa helped organize church classes for the Methodist Society and Jared was elected township treasurer and later justice of the peace.

The intersection where the family homestead still stands is

Jared and Louisa Rogers settled in a remote part of Barry County after emigrating from New York the year before statehood. The picture of Jared was made in the early 1850s, while that of Louisa was taken in front of the homestead at a reunion in about 1890. *Historic Charlton Park Village & Museum, Hastings*

known as Rogers Corners. The former school across the road was named for the family as well.

In 1844, Jared was appointed as local postmaster. His 13-year-old son Jeremiah carried the mail by horseback once a week between Hastings and Ionia. The youth's route was so isolated that there were no homes along a nine-mile stretch.

Jared was destined to make one more long journey, this one back to his native New York in 1854 to handle his father's estate.

He died there, far from his family and adopted home, and a newspaper obituary recorded, "He was taken sick with a complaint usual at this season and was soon hurried off the stage of action." The name of that fatal disease was not reported. His

Rogers Homestead. Descendants of Jared and Louisa Rogers gather for a 19th century reunion in front of the family homestead at Rogers Corners. To reach the site for the first time, Jared and two other men had to chop a road north from Hastings. *Kermit V. Washburn Sr.*

body was returned to Michigan and buried in the backyard of the homestead.

As for Jeremiah, the youthful postal courier grew up to become a farmer, agricultural implements merchant and buyer of livestock and grain, as well as a state legislator. A Republican, he was twice elected to the Michigan House of Representatives.

Silas Wheeler Rose Sr. and Margaret Myrtle

Howling wolves could be heard about his cabin at night.

"Few trails had been made and there were long distances between the clearings where a small field of grain would give proof of the enterprise of some hardy pioneer settler."

So it was in Clinton County in 1836 when Silas Wheeler Rose arrived with his wife and seven children.

"Howling wolves could be heard about his cabin at night and the friendly Indians made frequent visits to his home," according to a family account of their life and death in Michigan.

Silas was born in New York in 1802, the descendant of a Revolutionary War soldier who participated in the Battle of Bunker Hill and had fought under Gen. Benedict Arnold against the British in Canada. He met and wed Margaret Myrtle and then, at age 33, took the family west by way of the Erie Canal and by boat across Lake Erie to Detroit. Two more children would be born in Michigan.

Once they reached Michigan Territory, Silas bought an ox

Silas W. Rose Sr. and Margaret Myrtle Rose. Silas Rose Sr. was a politically active Democrat from his earliest days in what would become Bath Township, Clinton County, named for his hometown in New York. He helped lay out the roads and held several elective offices. He was serving as township clerk at the time of his death. Margaret outlived him by more than a half-century. Their graves are marked "Grandpa Silas" and Grandma Margaret." *Harold B. Burnett, History of Bath Charter Township*

team and initially settled in Washtenaw County, where he operated a hotel along the Detroit-to-Chicago stagecoach route.

From there it was north to what was then Ossowa Township, Clinton County, a lonely place of only five families, with the nearest neighbor three miles away. It was a "wild timber tract in the midst of the forest. . . . Only here and there would the smoke from a little cabin be seen, giving evidence that a clearing had been made and a home established in the woods," a township history relates. Silas was regarded as a good hunter, "able to furnish venison in plenty."

"He must have been a pretty dynamic person. He cut the first

SILAS WHEELER ROSE SR. & MARGARET MYRTLE

Silas W. Rose Jr. and Betty Fletcher Rose. Silas Jr. (*previous page*) arrived on the frontier as a child and married Betsy Fletcher, a fellow New Yorker. Betsy was active in church and community affairs. Her husband, a Republican unlike his father, held various township offices. As a local history put it, "He saw the great forests felled and the fields cleared and cultivated, saw the log cabins replaced with fine farm residences and little sheds for stock by commodious and substantial barns." *Harold B. Burnett, History of Bath Charter Township*

roads there," according to great-great-great granddaughter Beverly Harrison. She said Silas made trips to Pontiac for milling and trading, with each journey requiring a week of travel.

In 1839, Silas became the township's first supervisor. He later secured its redesignation as Bath Township, named for his home town in New York. By the time of his death in 1844, he had held

William H. Rose. The youngest of nine children, William Rose supplemented his log schoolhouse education with a politically active private tutor. He parlayed the original family farm to 515 acres, maintained real estate and lumbering businesses, and moved upward politically from township constable to county treasurer to state representative and ultimately to state land commissioner. *Harold B. Burnett, History of Bath Charter Township*

244

a variety of local offices, including justice of the peace, school inspector, pathmaster and director of the poor.

Although Silas died young, the widowed Margaret survived until age 99, spending the rest of her life on the farm with their youngest son William, who was active in real estate and lumbering. After Civil War service with the Michgan 15th Infantry Regiment, William was elected as Clinton County treasurer, as a two-term Republican member of the state House of Representatives and as state land commissioner.

Another son, "self-educated and self-made" Silas Jr. became township highway commissioner, constable, drain commissioner, treasurer and justice of the peace.

The family farm was later donated to the state and is now part of the Rose Lake Wildlife Research Area, operated by the Department of Natural Resources northeast of Lansing.

Trueman Sheldon and Susanna Knapp

Seeking better or cheaper land

Trueman Sheldon was older than most early settlers when he arrived on the frontier.

Already about 40, Trueman moved his family from Ontario to Lenawee County's Ogden Township, arriving with "considerable funds" to buy land. "Why they left Canada is not known, but probably like others in the East they were seeking better or cheaper land," a family history speculates.

Why southern Michigan?

"It is not improbable that land speculators and promoters of new settlements in the West were involved somewhere," the account suggests.

What was life like for Trueman and his wife Susanna Knapp when they arrived?

"At that time deer were plentiful, as well as wild turkeys, wolves and bears." Their six sons and two daughters were educated in a log school house on a neighbor's property, learning their lessons on "rough homemade benches."

Susanna and Trueman were successful. Land records show they bought their first farm in 1836, then went on to acquire other large holdings in the township. Their original log house gave way to frame buildings.

Like his parents, son Harvey also felt a westward urge. He ventured to California during the gold rush and spent four years as a miner before returning to Michigan to farm.

Susanna's death in 1864 and a family furor over Trueman's subsequent remarriage prompted Trueman to leave his adopted state. He married Virginia-born widow Sarah Wilmouth, triggering what the family account diplomatically described as "some unpleasantness" between him and his children.

"It probably created a scandal around here. They probably figured she was after his money, and they didn't like it, so he got mad and took off," said great-great-great grandson James J. Sheldon. James noted that Sarah was undoubtedly much younger than her new husband.

Trueman sold his property southeast of Adrian, gave a farm to each of his adult sons and moved west to Missouri with his bride in 1868. He was seen leaving town walking behind a wagon, carrying a rifle. The couple had four children in Missouri before Trueman's death in 1881.

Moses Wisner and Eliza Richardson

Cheerfully gave up the honors and peaceful pursuits of the citizen to undergo the hardships and privations of the soldier's life

Moses Wisner's service to his adopted state came to a tragic end when typhoid fever struck the ranks of Union troops and claimed the former governor's life in 1863.

But during the 26 preceding years, Moses left a major mark on Michigan as a lawyer and politician.

He arrived in Michigan from New York in 1837, the year of statehood, and bought a farm in Lapeer County. He gave up farming after two years to study law, then became county prosecutor before moving to Pontiac.

Moses was not the first Wisner to come west. His older brother George had moved to Pontiac in 1835 after helping to establish the *New York Sun*. George also studied law, was elected to a term in the state House of Representatives, served as Oakland County prosecutor and became editor of the *Detroit Advertiser*. A biography described George as "a leading Whig, a fine lawyer, an eloquent speaker in a political campaign (who) held a

Moses Wisner, a founder of the Michigan Republican Party, defeated Democrat Charles Stuart to win the governorship in 1858. His tenure was marked by compulsory voter registration, expansion of roads, anti-slavery activism, and advocacy for the admission of women into the University of Michigan. Before the Civil War erupted, he vigorously criticized the intent of the South to secede, saying, "We cannot consent to have one star obliterated from our flag." *State Archives of Michigan*

leading place in the remembrance of the pioneers of Oakland County."

Moses first wife, Eliza Richardson, died in childbirth in 1844. Four years later, he married Angeolina Hascall, the daughter of a prominent early settler who owned the first printing press in Pontiac and the first hotel in Auburn. Angeolina's father Charles served on the Territorial Council and in the Senate before statehood, was a militia general in the Toledo War and founded the *Flint Republican.*

Initially an anti-slavery Whig, Moses helped establish the Michigan Republican Party at its organizational meeting in Jackson and waged unsuccessful campaigns as its candidate for Congress in 1854 and for the U.S. Senate in 1857.

It was in 1858 that he won the governorship. His term was marked by the construction of roads into still-unsettled parts of the state.

As he left office on New Year's Day 1861, secession and war loomed on the horizon due to the recent election of fellow

Pine Grove. Moses Wisner's Pine Grove home in Pontiac was built in 1845 along the old Saginaw Trail and served as the governor's office and official residence during most of his tenure as Michigan's chief executive. He entertained there because his $1,000 salary was inadequate to maintain a proper social life in Lansing. The home got its name because Wisner planted a variety of types of native Michigan pines on the property. It is now a registered historic site and serves as headquarters for the Oakland County Pioneer and Historical Society. *Oakland County Pioneer and Historical Society*

Republican Abraham Lincoln. "This is no time for timid and vacillating counsels when the cry of treason and rebellion is ringing in our ears," he declared in his farewell address.

After the Civil War broke out, Moses organized the 22d Michigan Infantry Regiment and, as its colonel, led his troops to Lexington, Ky. He fell fatally ill with typhoid before the regiment, made up largely of Oakland County soldiers, saw battle. Angeolina rushed to Kentucky to stay with her husband until he died.

250

Announcing his death, Army Gen. G. Granger wrote: "When his country called for men to fight her battles, he cheerfully gave up the honors and peaceful pursuit of the citizen to undergo the hardships and privations of the soldier's life."

As a biography later stated, "His eloquence was that of conviction and action, and the people believed in him."

William P. Bristol and Deborah Marshall

The neighbors were not close enough for the chickens to scratch up each other's grain.

It could have been considered a bad omen when William P. Bristol's covered wagon tipped over and dumped part of its load while fording Wabascon Creek near Battle Creek.

William and his wife Deborah Marshall were undaunted, however, although that region of the Michigan Territory in 1837 was far more remote and challenging than New York. They continued on to a sparsely settled part of Barry County. As one account described the area: "The neighbors were not close enough for the chickens to scratch up each other's grain so there were no neighborhood quarrels."

Before moving permanently to the frontier, William had hired an uncle to build a house and clear a field for corn, but the uncle abandoned the task after his only plow was smashed – the nearest replacement being 26 miles away in Marshall – and after a brush fire destroyed a load of hay and the hay wagon, according to local history.

William and Deborah Bristol found an unexpected and unwelcome surprise when they arrived in Barry County — the house they expected to be ready hadn't been built yet. Even so, they were not discouraged enough to turn back. *Historic Charlton Park Village & Museum, Hastings*

The couple therefore arrived to find no home ready. With winter fast approaching, William "hastily cut the logs, went to the neighbors and got help."

One of their lasting legacies is M-37, the main road linking Hastings with Battle Creek. William was influential in getting what was then called the Western Road built. The new road passed through Johnstown Township, which he helped organize, and, not surprisingly, ran right by his property.

There he opened a tavern, first in a log house and then in a 2 ½-story Greek revival-style building with curved rafters, a dining room, ladies' parlor and sleeping quarters. The Bristols' tav-

The Bristol Inn was a popular mid-Michigan stopping point for stage-coaches until competition and rising taxes made the business unprofitable and forced its closure. The Greek revival-style building was moved to the historic village in Hastings' Charlton Park, where it was restored and is now open to visitors. *Michigan Travel Commission*

ern and inn became a popular breakfast stop for the Good Intent Stagecoach Line, which traveled along the Western Road.

He also maintained the local post office in his home to service nearby settlers, and opened a blacksmith shop that could be used by the stagecoach drivers.

In 1862, high liquor taxes and competition from a newer neighboring tavern, the Robinson House, forced William out of the tavernkeeping business, but he became a successful farmer. For many years the former inn remained a landmark in the now-defunct community of Bristolville, 15 miles south of Hastings.

William's brother Elias also settled in Michigan before state-

Stagecoach line ad. Good Intent stagecoach routes ran between Kalamazoo, Battle Creek and Grand Rapids and stopped at the tavern operated by the Bristol family. The company, which helped make central and western Michigan more accessible to the state and the nation, prided itself on "good horses, new coaches and careful and experienced drivers." *State Archives of Michigan*

hood. Elias originally chose Lenawee County, where he ran a tavern and fished commercially before joining William in Johnstown Township.

On the political front, William helped form the township government. The first municipal election was held in his house, where 12 of the 13 initial voters present were chosen for public office. Over the years he served as justice of the peace, supervisor and "path master," a job that involved staking out new roads. He also hosted the inaugural meeting of the local Grange.

Sesquicentennial Pioneer Program

To help celebrate Michigan's Sesquicentennial — the 150th anniversary of statehood on Jan. 6, 1987 — the Michigan Genealogical Council and Library of Michigan designed a program to honor descendants of early residents, both Native American and settlers. The goal was twofold: to recognize people who shaped Michigan and to preserve information about them and the way they lived.

Under the program, direct descendants could qualify for a Sesquicentennial Pioneer certificate by proving that an ancestor had lived in Michigan, even for a short time, by Dec. 31, 1837. They also were required to document each subsequent generation from that ancestor to themselves. Almost 8,000 applications were received for thousands of ancestors.

The first certificate was awarded to Paula Parker Blanchard, then the wife of Gov. James J. Blanchard, who is a great-great-great granddaughter of Oakland County pioneer Walter Knox.

Sesquicentennial symbol

Knox was born near Edinburgh, Scotland, in 1799 and came to upstate New York in 1832. Walter and his wife Jane Todd settled in Pontiac in 1836, then moved to the wilderness of Independence Township. Of their experiences, a county history says:

> The long journey was made under the difficulties which met the pioneers of that day. They settled on uncleared land, far from any depot of supplies, while the only cattle that could be used to advantage were the strong but slow-moving oxen. On many occasions, Mr. Knox walked many miles to get his grist of meal ground. He cleared up a fine farm with the assistance of his sons, and put it under cultivation, his death preventing his long enjoyment of the fruit of his labors.

The final Sesquicentennial Pioneer certificates were awarded to descendants of Ira Foster Jr. of New York, who visited Keeler Township, Van Buren County, in 1836 and returned the following year with his wife Sarah Ann Rowe and their son in an ox-drawn wagon. "When he came here, there was not even an

258

The Library of Michigan and The Michigan Genealogical Council
proudly presents

Michigan's Sesquicentennial Pioneer Certificate

to

in recognition of

The Contribution of a Pioneer Ancestor

who settled in the State of Michigan prior to December 31, 1837

Presented at Lansing, Michigan

this _____ day of _____ 198__

State Librarian, Library of Michigan

President, Michigan Genealogical Council

Sesquicentennial Pioneer certificate. Applicants who proved that an ancestor had lived in Michigan by 1837 received certificates "in recognition of the contribution of a pioneer ancestor." *Library of Michigan*

Library of Michigan

Library of Michigan and Michigan Genealogical Council. The Library of Michigan and the Michigan Genealogical Council cosponsored the Sesquicentennial Pioneer program. The library, an arm of the Legislature, is one of the largest and most comprehensive state libraries in the nation. The council, formed in 1972, coordinates the activities of more than 70 genealogical societies across the state.

Indian trail on his place anywhere," according to a county history. When Sarah died in 1839 of "pioneer exposure," Ira left the child with a neighbor, "walked back to New York, bought another ox team, married a second wife and returned to the log cabin built for Sarah."

In Search of
Michigan Roots

Margaret C. Bator's search for her Michigan heritage began at an antique booth when she chanced upon an old history book about St. Joseph County. Out of curiosity, she checked through the volume and came across an account about her great-great grandfather, Orsamus Cook Merill Bates, who had emigrated from New York in 1833 and developed what the book called a "handsome and highly improved farm" in Constantine. Bator became hooked on family history.

For Larry L. Blackett, the search for his Michigan roots also began accidentally. On a visit to the Chickamauga battlefield in Tennessee, he remembered how the future son-in-law of ancestor Austin N. Kimmis Sr., a 19th century Oakland County sheriff, had fought in the Civil War. When he returned home, Blackett began to research his family and discovered that Kimmis' son-in-law was captured by Confederate troops at Chickamauga and spent 18 months in the notorious Andersonville prison in Georgia.

Happenstance is not the only way to spark an interest in family history. Another is oral tradition, listening to family tales as they are passed on from generation to generation.

For example, as a child Valma Marie Freytag Kelly visited her great-grandfather Toussaint Champagne, who had been born in Monroe County the year of statehood. "My mother always talked about the huge table Toussaint's wife had for Thanksgiving. It was laden with all kinds of good stuff, not one kind of potato but two or three, and all kinds of pies," she recalled. Toussaint's own great-grandfather, Montreal-born Pierre Huyet dit Champagne, was in Michigan at least as early as 1760, when he married in Detroit.

Similarly, Mary Roma Nowak's interest in tracing her ancestors, Kalamazoo County settlers Luther and Sarah Pond, began in childhood. "It was a natural inclination, I guess," she said. "I'd get my uncles talking about the family."

Other people get hooked through school projects or community historical celebrations. One is Yvonne Marie Peer, who started researching her great-great-great-great grandfather Shawano, a Chippewa chief from Sault Ste. Marie, for a college paper. "I knew I was a little bit Indian and casually asked about living descendants of Shawano," she said.

Still others are fascinated by such mysteries and puzzles as missing limbs on the family tree or unidentified faces in yellowing snapshots or dusty portraits. Filling in the pieces can be like solving a jigsaw puzzle.

Dorothy Shane had long been interested in family history but was unaware that her ancestor Samuel Babcock, a settler in Jackson and St. Joseph counties, had been married twice. She learned of the first marriage when she came across his name while checking for something else in an Oakland County census record. That discovery took her to Detroit to research the 1832 cholera epidemic in which Babcock's first wife and four children died.

On a national level, more and more people are reaching out to touch their past. The search for heritage makes genealogy an increasingly popular pastime — some would say compulsion.

Roots-mania has inspired heritage hunting expeditions, lengthy conversations with family elders and courses in family and local history. High school and college students come home from class to interview their grandparents for reports. Grandparents research the past to preserve a legacy for their grandchildren's future.

There are many primary and secondary sources for researching your Michigan roots. Here are the principal ones:

• Official birth, marriage and death records are available from 1867 on from the clerk of the county where the event occurred or from the Michigan Department of Public Health, Box 30035, Lansing MI 48909.

• Census records were compiled for the 1820 and 1830 territorial censuses, for the federal census every 10 years starting in 1840 and ending in 1910, and for state censuses in 1834, 1845, 1854, 1864, 1874, 1884, 1894 and 1904. Many state census records were lost over time and are not available, however. Censuses also were conducted during French and British colonial rule.

• Wills, estate records and guardianship records are filed in Probate Court. Most counties have their own Probate Court, although there are some multi-county probate districts. The State Archives of Michigan in Lansing and Western Michigan University also have probate records for some counties.

• Land records and plats are available in the county where the property is owned, generally in the office of the register of deeds. In addition to showing real estate transactions, these records often include marital relationships and residency. The State Archives has other land documents, including indexes to land sales, records of homestead lands, original surveyor maps dating to 1815, private claims surveys and abstracts of land grants for property received or sold by the state.

• Tax records date back to the time each county was formed and are filed with the county treasurer or register of deeds. The State Archives, Western Michigan University and Michigan Technological University also maintain some county and township tax and assessment rolls.

• Military records are available from the National Archives & Records Service, 8th & Pennsylvania Ave. N.W., Washington, DC 20408 and the State Archives. They include muster-in and muster-out records, pay vouchers, military bounty land warrants and pension papers for the Revolutionary War (1775–1783); War of 1812 (1812–1815); Mexican-American War (1845–1849); Indian and other wars (1816–1898); Civil War (1861–1865); Spanish-American War (1898–1899); and World War I (1914–1918). Most major Michigan libraries maintain a 46-volume index of Civil War soldiers from the state that lists name, rank, date and place of enlistment, physical description and other data.

The State Archives also maintains a Civil War graves registration index; records of the Grand Army of the Republic and United Spanish War Veterans; files on residents of the state Soldier and Sailors' Home for indigent veterans and their dependents; and some county and local records on draftees, volunteers, burials, prisoners of war and civil defense volunteers. The Michigan National Guard maintains public records about former members of the Guard.

• Civil War manuscripts, primarily letters and diaries by Michigan soldiers, are at the State Archives.

• Church records generally include birth, baptism, death, marriage and funeral information.

• Education records from public schools often include attendance and grade books, school directories and minutes of school board meetings.

264

• Rural property inventories for 1.5 million parcels of real estate were conducted from 1935 to 1942 during the Depression under sponsorship of the federal Works Progress Administration and the State Tax Commission. They include descriptions of land, buildings, fences, crops, sources of heat and light, woodlots and other information, with sketches of the houses and general land area. Most are held at the State Archives, although Michigan Technological University has the inventories for three Upper Peninsula counties.

• Cemetery and mortuary records and tombstone inscriptions. The Library of Michigan has mapped 3,800 cemeteries in the state and has transcriptions for many tombstones.

• Burial and transport permits are filed in county health departments or village, township and city halls.

• Court records date back to each county's formation. They cover civil litigation, criminal cases, divorce proceedings and naturalization.

• Corporate annual reports dating to 1847 are held at the State Archives and include such information as the names of directors, financial data and, sometimes, names and addresses of shareholders with their holdings. The Corporation and Securities Bureau also maintains corporate records.

• Naturalization records include such information as date and place of birth, country of origin, date and port of immigration, physical description and occupation. The State Archives has naturalization records dating to 1835 for some counties, while Western Michigan University Archives has them for two counties in the southwestern part of the state.

• Legislative papers from standing and special committees of the Michigan House of Representatives and Senate are filed in the State Archives.

• Prison records include physical descriptions of inmates, terms, reasons for incarceration, escape attempts, birth date, educational and occupational background, personal habits, previous criminal history, parole and discharge dates and, sometimes, photos dating to 1839. They are held at the State Archives.

- State reformatory records dating to 1856 for boys and 1881 for girls are on file at the State Archives. They include case studies and biographical information.
- Election records dating to 1819 are in the State Archives. They include county canvasser statements, election nominations and ballots, election return statistics on a statewide basis, as well as some county, city and township election records.
- Family bibles may list births, marriages, deaths and other significant events involving relatives.
- Records from county and state poor homes, santitoriums and infirmaries include patient registers, medical files and inspection reports. They are available at the State Archives. However, mental health records after 1859 that pertain to specific patients are confidential and can be examined only upon application.
- Newspaper articles and obituaries. Local libraries generally keep copies of community newspapers. A wider range of old newspapers is available on microfilm at the Library of Michigan, large public libraries and major universities.
- Family histories and genealogies – some sketchy and other detailed – were written by relatives and sometimes published. The Library of Michigan has an extensive statewide collection. Local libraries and historical societies often have some local genealogies.
- County histories or portrait and biographical history books were published for virtually every county in the late 19th and early 20th centuries. They can be found at the Library of Michigan, local libraries and historical societies and universities.
- City and county directories are available at the Library of Michigan and local libraries. The first was published in Detroit in 1837, and the second city to have one was Grand Rapids in 1859.

• Personal papers, including journals, diaries, letters and family reunion reports.

• Atlases and landowner plat books can be found in the Library of Michigan and local libraries.

• Records of centennial farms, owned by the same family for at least 100 years, are maintained by the Bureau of History in the Secretary of State's office.

In addition, the State Archives has specialized collections for genealogical and historical research. Among them are:

• Native American records dating to 1818. They include maps, documents and reports about land, schools, Indian agents, government commissions and tribal affairs.

• African-American records dating to 1818. They include reports and documents about slavery, military service, government studies, segregation and education.

• Mining records of various Michigan companies and state agencies dating to 1817. They include studies and surveys, appraisals and production figures.

• Railroad records compiled by state agencies dating to 1833. Among them are company annual reports, assessment rolls, records of rate cases and land claims.

• Logging and forestry records dating to 1850. They include records of individual lumbering companies, state timber assessments, news clippings, correspondence, forest fire reports, log marks and liens.

• Records of professions registered or licensed by the counties or state are on file at the State Archives. The earliest — for merchants, peddlers, ferry masters, auctioneers and tavern keepers — date to 1837.

• Depression-era agency records for the Civilian Conservation Corps, Federal Emergency Relief Administration, National Youth Administration, Work Projects Administration and state Planning Commission are kept at the State Archives. These include information on participants, correspondence, contracts and reports.

- Photo files are kept in the State Archives. The collection has more than 330,000 images.
- Maps, about 500,000 of them, are also in the State Archives.

Local historical and genealogical societies, museums and libraries are good sources of guidance and information. For a directory of the member societies of the Michigan Genealogical Council, send $1 plus a self-addressed stamped envelope to Michigan Genealogical Council, Liaison Office, Library of Michigan, Box 30007, Lansing MI 48909. Many of the societies publish newsletters and community histories. The Library of Michigan also houses the council's Michigan Surname Index, containing more than 100,000 entries.

Other major research resources are found at the Burton Historical Collection of the Detroit Public Library; Waldo Library at Western Michigan University; Clarke Historical Library at Central Michigan University; the Bentley Historical Library at the University of Michigan; and the Reynolds Historical Genealogy Collection at the Allen County Public Library in Fort Wayne, Ind.

A helpful reference guide to available county records, office hours and search fees is Michigan Genealogy: Sources & Resources by Carol McGinnis (Genealogical Publishing Co., Baltimore, 1987). The book also lists library and museum genealogical collections; Michigan branches of the Genealogical Libraries of the Church of Jesus Christ of Latter Day Saints (Mormons); and historical and genealogical societies.

The Michigan Museum Guide, published by the Michigan Museums Association, is available from the Michigan Travel Bureau, Box 30226, Lansing MI 48909. Many of the museums have historical collections.

Warning: Genealogical research can mushroom from casual interest to intensive effort. As an illustration, William A. McQueen, a descendant of original Detroit settlers Francis Bienvenu dit DeLisle and his wife Geneveva Charon dit La Ferriere, wrote:

> The first knowledge of the family history was received through conversation. As time went on curiosity was increased as family records such as pictures and scrapbooks were made available. A whole new window into the family history was opened when the Detroit Society for Genealogical Research and the Burton Historical Collection of the Detroit Public Library as a bicentennial project published the two-volume 'Genealogy of French Families of the Detroit River Region 1701–1911.' Excited by this new information I soon read and collected books of Michigan and Detroit history. Joining the Detroit Society for Genealogical Research directed me toward other sources of information. In 1982 they published 'Michigan Censuses 1710–1830.' This is another source of bits and pieces of information that help fill in pieces of the puzzle that has an infinite number of pieces.

Is it worth the effort? As McQueen put it:

> The more we learn, the more we expand our interest. What was life really like for our pioneer families? Frequent infant deaths, severe weather with little protection, plagues with 20 percent of the population afflicted. Building your house by hand, the tables and chairs, making your clothes, growing your own food.
> Being a descendant of a pioneer family gives one a feeling of possession and pride. While driving a crowded freeway or walking in a remote wooded area of our state, one constantly thinks about our history and the lives of our ancestors. There is so much more to be discovered and recorded.

AUTHOR

Eric Freedman, an award-winning reporter for *The Detroit News*, graduated from Cornell University and New York University School of Law. He worked as an aide to U.S. Rep. Charles B. Rangel of New York, then began his journalism career at the Albany (N.Y.) *Knickerbocker News*. In 1984, he joined *The Detroit News* Capitol Bureau in Lansing and is on the adjunct faculty at Michigan State University's Journalism Department. He also is author of *On the Water, Michigan*, a comprehensive guide to water recreation in the state, and his freelance articles have appeared in dozens of U.S. and Canadian newspapers and magazines.

Index

Mackinaw City, Emmet County 27, 85, 92, 141, 147
Mackinaw State Forest 142–143
Manwaring, Adam 235–237
Manwaring, Ella 237
Manwaring, George 235
Manwaring, Joseph 236–237
Manwaring, Joshua 236
Manwaring, Susan Platt 235–237
Maple Grove 102
Marquette, Marquette County 173
Marquette, Chief 95
Marquette, Jacques 26
Marshall, Calhoun County 252
Marshall Statesman 224
Mason, Ingham County 232
Mason, Emily V. 21
Mason, John 23
Mason, Marcia Van Auken 134
Mason, Stevens T. 21–23, 38, 59, 111, 187
Mathewson, Welcome 51
Maumee River 21–22, 25
McGinnis, Carol 268
McGulpin, Madeleine Crequi 91
McGulpin, Madeline Bourassa 90, 92
McGulpin, Patrick 91
McGulpin, William 89–92
McGulpin House 89–90
McGulpin's Point Lighthouse 92
McQueen, William A. 77, 269
Meldrum, Angelique Mary Catherine Chapoton 84–88
Meldrum, George 84–88
Menominees 25, 47
Methodist Society 238
Mexican-American War 264
Miamis 25, 47
Michigan Corporation & Securities Bureau 265

Michigan Genealogical Council 15, 257–260, 268
"Michigan Genealogy: Sources & Resources" 268
Michigan Museums Association 268
Michigan National Guard 264
Michigan Pioneer & Historical Society 71
Michigan Public Health Department 263
Michigan State University 236
Michigan Technological University 264–265
"Michigania" 65–67
Michilmackinac 25, 93
Milford Township, Oakland County 199
Millar, John 50
Monroe, Monroe County 14, 35–36, 96–98, 146–147, 177–180, 191
Monroe, James 44, 86, 96
Monroe Democrat 35
Monroe Township, Monroe County 144
Morris, Charles 126–129
Morris, Dolphin 124–129
Morris, Esther 126–129
Morris, Lewis 126
Morris, Samuel 124
Morris, Susanna Nancy Beaver 124–129
Mt. Clemens, Macomb County 133
Mundy Township, Genesee County 183–184
Muskegon River 110

Napoleon 181–182

278

279

Index